TWENTIETH CENTURY VIEWS

The aim of this series is to present the best in contemporary critical opinion on major authors, providing a twentieth century perspective on their changing status in an era of profound revaluation.

Maynard Mack, *Series Editor*
Yale University

THE AMERICAN
AUTOBIOGRAPHY

A COLLECTION OF CRITICAL ESSAYS

Edited by
Albert E. Stone

Prentice-Hall, Inc. A SPECTRUM BOOK *Englewood Cliffs, N.J.*

Library of Congress Cataloging in Publication Data
Main entry under title:

The American autobiography.

(Twentieth century views) (A Spectrum Book)
Bibliography: p.
1. American literature—History and
criticism—Addresses, essays, lectures.
2. Autobiography—Addresses, essays, lectures.
I. Stone, Albert E.   II. Series.
PS169.A95A5   810'.9'351   81-10530
                                              AACR2

ISBN 0-13-024638-7

ISBN 0-13-024620-4 {PBK.}

Editorial/production supervision by Alberta Boddy
Cover illustration by Vivian Berger
Manufacturing buyer: Barbara A. Frick

10 9 8 7 6 5 4 3 2 1

PRENTICE-HALL INTERNATIONAL, INC. *(London)*
PRENTICE-HALL OF AUSTRALIA PTY. LIMITED *(Sydney)*
PRENTICE-HALL OF CANADA, LTD. *(Toronto)*
PRENTICE-HALL OF INDIA PRIVATE LIMITED *(New Delhi)*
PRENTICE-HALL OF JAPAN, INC. *(Tokyo)*
PRENTICE-HALL OF SOUTHEAST ASIA PTE. LTD. *(Singapore)*
WHITEHALL BOOKS LIMITED *Wellington, (New Zealand)*

Contents

Acknowledgments

The quotation from *The Letters of Sigmund Freud and Arnold Zweig.* Reprinted by permission of Harcourt Brace Jovanovich, the publishers, and Sigmund Freud Copyrights Ltd. (11/12 West Stockwell Street, Colchester, UK CO1 18N).

Quotations from A.Berkman, *Prison Memoirs of an Anarchist.* Reprinted from the New York Schocken Books, Inc., 1970.

Quotations from Mary Antin, *The Promised Land.* Reprinted by permission of the publishers, Houghton Mifflin Company.

Scattered quotes from Zora Neale Hurston, *Dust Tracks on a Road;* Richard Wright, *Black Boy;* and Abraham Cahan, *The Rise of David Levinksy.* Reprinted by permission of Harper & Row, Publishers, Inc.

Quotations from Ronald Sanders, *Reflections on a Teapot: The Personal History of a Time.* Reprinted by permission of Georges Borchardt, Inc., 1972.

Excerpts from Charles Mingus and Nel King, *Beneath the Underdog.* Used by permission of the Estate of Charles Mingus.

Scattered quotes from Leroi Jones, *Blues People.* Reprinted by permission of William Morrow & Co.

Quotations from Taylor Gordon, *Born to Be.* Reprinted by permission of The University of Washington Press, Seattle, Washington.

Quotations from Charley White and Ada Holland, *No Quittin' Sense.* Reprinted by permission of The University of Texas Press, Austin, Texas.

Scattered quotes from *Soledad Brother: The Prison Letters of George Jackson.* Published by Coward, McCann & Geogphegan and Bantam Books, Inc. Copyright ©1970 by World Entertainers Limited. By permission of Bantam Books, Inc. All rights reserved.

Scattered quotes from Alfred Kazin, *A Walker in the City;* Irving Howe, *Steady Work* and *Decline of the New;* Claude McKay, *A Long Way From Home: An Autobiography.* Reprinted by permission of Harcourt Brace Jovanovich, Inc.

Excerpts from Theodore Rosengarten, *All God's Dangers: The Life of Nate Shaw.* Reprinted by permission of Alfred A. Knopf, 1974.

Excerpts from Maya Angelou, *I Know Why the Caged Bird Sings.* Reprinted by permission of Random House, 1970.

Excerpts from Ralph Ellison, *Shadow and Act.* Reprinted by permission of Random House, 1964.

Chapter opening quote, Alfred Kazin, "The Self as History," from Albert Camus, *The Stranger,* translated by Stuart Gilbert. Reprinted by permission of Alfred A. Knopf, 1946.

Introduction: American Autobiographies as Individual Stories and Cultural Narratives

by Albert E. Stone

One of the notable cultural developments in recent decades is the remarkable flowering of American autobiography, not only as a major mode of literary self-expression, but also as a widely popular form of reading and an important new field for scholars and critics. To be sure, personal narratives have long occupied an acknowledged niche in American literature. Well before the paperback revolution, readers were familiar with the names and life-stories of Franklin, Thoreau, and Whitman, as of Henry Adams, Gertrude Stein, and Richard Wright. But to these names and titles are now added a host of new ones. Autobiographies in surprising numbers are available today in drugstores and supermarkets as in libraries and bookstores. The recent phenomenon of *Roots*, both as "faction" and as a smash hit on television, attests to the fascination personal history holds for Americans of many ages, classes, races, and sexes. Our curiosity about each other's lives produces a steady stream of merely topical successes as well as some contemporary classics like *Black Elk Speaks* and *The Autobiography of Malcolm X*, Lillian Hellman's *Pentimento*, and Maxine Hong Kingston's *The Woman Warrior.* The great variety of forms chosen to re-create a self in prose indicates the flexibility of the autobiographical mode. Writing one's life history, in this day of the tape recorder and the ghostwriter, is an outlet available to the illiterate and the educated, the newcomer and the Native American, the unknown young and the famous old. As Robert Sayre observes, autobiographies are a Song of Ourselves composed of thousands of Songs of Myself. The nature and cultural significance of this rich and characteristically American mode of storytelling is the subject of this collection of critical essays.

1

As "the most democratic province in the republic of letters" (p. 798),* autobiography indeed mirrors and creates the social, historical, and aesthetic varieties of our national experience. The phrase is William Dean Howells's; it appeared in 1909 in *Harper's Monthly Magazine*, exactly a century after the word "autobiography" was first coined in England. Himself an autobiographer as well as a novelist and critic, Howells was one of the first and most enthusiastic devotees of American autobiography. Long before Gusdorf, Pascal, Cox, Hart, Olney, Weintraub, and the other influential critics whom Sayre cites, Howells recognized autobiography's complex nature and varied social uses. In the language of psychoanalysis, autobiography is, in fact, an overdetermined document; it is simultaneously historical record and literary artifact, psychological case history and spiritual confession, didactic essay and ideological testament. Uniting all these available modes and possible motives for "telling one's story" is, of course, the self who is both actor and author. Personal identity is the root and result of the autobiographical act. Therefore, autobiography brings life to literature, as Janet Varner Gunn asserts. Hence, most of the compartments of public and private experience which in Western cultures have been organized into the social sciences and humanities are relevant to autobiography. The selections included here, and the bibliography which pieces out their inevitable sketchiness, reflect this complex cultural status. Together, these essays and books, whose number and range argue eloquently for the current interest in this subject, suggest fruitful approaches by historians, literary critics, psychologists, and other social scientists, as well as by scholars in American Studies, Afro-American Studies, and Women's Studies. No single disciplinary perspective, I would argue, embraces or explains so protean an activity of self-construction. Autobiographical narratives, therefore, are a naturally interdisciplinary subject.

For critics as for the common reader, the best place to start to understand autobiography as a cultural act is with history. The deep impulse to tell one's story as a creature of one time and place, to reveal how one's existence has been "circumstanced," as Howells puts it, is a fundamental feature that Sayre, Kazin, Spacks, Doherty, Schultz, and Rosenfeld each attributes to modern autobiography. Wary present-day readers might balk at Wilhelm Dilthey's confident, turn-of-the-

---

*Page references in this introduction are to the works cited in the Selected Bibliography at the end of the book.

century assertion that autobiography is *the* history-making act, and represents "the highest and most instructive form in which the understanding of life confronts us" (p. 85). Nevertheless, Kazin correctly defines a central American tradition when he calls autobiography "the self living history." Expressing vividly one's relationship to the past is a *personal* though not necessarily a *private* act, as both Kazin and Francis Russell Hart point out. A historical consciousness speaks *out of* singular experience, *for* some particular social group, *to* a wider audience. This triple articulation is at once an act of perception and creation: what forces in the past have made me, how I now see and express my unique individuality. Autobiography is, simply and profoundly, personal history.

A useful way to investigate the varieties of historical consciousness represented in two centuries of American autobiography is to place Sayre's and Kazin's eloquent descriptions in the broader context of Western cultural history. Patricia Meyer Spacks does this by agreeing with Sayre's treatment of autobiography as a history of changing self-concepts. By locating American texts in a larger European context, she shows that our culture's fascination with certain stages of human development—especially with childhood, adolescence, and young adulthood—is itself a historical phenomenon. Other cultures and earlier centuries have their privileged periods of life in terms of which the autobiographer decides to present the self's story. The very concept of the life cycle, Spacks suggests, and the successive psychosocial crises out of which a mature identity emerges, is a "necessary fiction." At any moment, autobiography may be viewed as a collection of such acts of self-performance unified by shared cultural values and fashionable metaphors of the self. Women's perceptions of these crucial stages will differ from men's, however, just as period, class, economic, and racial factors influence one's choice of childhood, youth, or maturity as the vital center of a narrative. Thus Spacks historicizes autobiography as a literary act of dramatic self-performance. She seems to deny, however, to stages of the life cycle any priority or objective status as universal categories of experience or identity. For a different counterpointing of autobiography, culture, and psychosocial theory, one should read Erik Erikson and Bruce Mazlish. "Gandhi's Autobiography: The Leader as a Child" shows a particularly deft use of psychoanalytic generalizations. Erikson sees all autobiography expressing the psychosocial development of an individual, the historical moments in which that process unfolds, and the literary choices of the author who retrospectively presents and interprets their interaction.

History and social circumstance are presences of special power in black American autobiographies. As Elizabeth Schultz points out, this has been a truism since the time of the ante-bellum slave narratives. Indeed, many oppressed groups and individuals have turned to personal history as a means of understanding and protesting against the social realities which have decisively affected their lives and identities. Schultz's description of black autobiography as a double tradition of the testimonial record and the blues performance— embracing, for example, *Up From Slavery* and *The Autobiography of W.E.B. Du Bois* as well as *Black Boy* and *I Know Why The Caged Bird Sings*—does not lessen the force of historical consciousness. Black autobiography is thoroughly, inexorably historical; as Roger Rosenblatt observes, "no black American author has ever felt the need to invent a nightmare to make his point" (p. 171). Whether as polemic or parable, as bare recital of events or rich oral performance, black autobiography vividly re-creates links between the singular self, the immediate community, and a wider world of sympathetic readers and fellow human beings. *The Autobiography of Malcom X*, by combining the testimonial and blues traditions and techniques, occupies a central place today as an exemplary American life story. It is, moreover, a triumph of collaborative art.

The sense that history sets the terms for autobiography is likewise strong in other traditions, including those of immigrants and American Jews. Alvin Rosenfeld's essay, tracing the trajectory of Jewish autobiography from early twentieth-century beginnings to present-day experiments, rests upon such awareness, both in the writers themselves and in the critic. Mary Antin's *The Promised Land* dramatizes the historical experience of Americanization in frankly mythic terms. She presents herself as the prototypical immigrant transformed into a new self by changes of name, clothing, language, and religion. Antin and Kazin are first- and second-generation Jews escaping from Jewish history and culture. Kazin's embrace of a native American past, both Christian and literary, in *A Walker in the City* (and in his essay reprinted here) constitutes for Rosenfeld a betrayal of the Jewish past and pious tradition. Podhoretz, Sanders, Gold, and Ozick, though less familiar names than Antin's or Kazin's, exemplify better the contemporary situation: American Jews telling their story as practicing believers again, Yiddish speakers, devotees of family obligations and patriarchal ties.

Rosenfeld's impassioned account takes for granted explicit ideology in authorial consciousnesses and in the critic of autobiography as well. Thomas Doherty's examination of American autobiography and ideology likewise highlights the powerful influence of a pervasive secular individualism, typified classically in *The Autobiography of Benjamin Franklin*. Against this consensus belief many autobiographers have (literally) pitted themselves. George Jackson's *Soledad Brother* and Alexander Berkman's *Prison Memoirs of an Anarchist* are juxtaposed in order to demonstrate the tensions which can arise between specific ideological commitments and the impulse toward self-construction in writing. Doherty concludes by questioning the fundamental implications of autobiography in America. The concept of an individual, developing self which lies at the core of autobiography often runs counter to beliefs arising from historical and social realities. Thus autobiography is at once a revolutionary and a conservative document. A voice—Black Elk's, say, or Nate Shaw's—tells of previously unknown experiences and cultural values. In the process, a distinctive self is forged, subtly separate from and occasionally antagonistic to its own ideological assertions. In this struggle, Doherty suggests, autobiography in America often overpowers dissenting outlooks.

Ideologies, like autobiography itself, give shape and meaning to historical memories. Both are necessary fictions. At the same time, an ideology meets deep emotional needs for the believer whose identity, as Erikson argues, is confirmed by acts of allegiance. Locating the self within time, community, and a system of thought is, however, simply one available mode of self-construction. *Walden* represents another exemplary strategy. It discovers the self in nature more than within nineteenth-century American history and society. Thoreau's book is a spiritual re-creation and language act which reconstitutes its artificer in terms of a specific place and within a fully temporal setting. The deepest dimensions of Thoreau's individuality are uncovered in acts of gazing, sauntering, speaking his myriad relationships to the universe in the shape of Walden Pond, a thawing sand bank, a bean field, the return of geese in spring. Autobiography in these terms is no mere historical record of human events and relationships but a personal synonym and synecdoche of reality. If one's true depth is reflected in nature, then the self is properly re-created in a fully imaginative act of reading, not simply of writing. Such is Janet Varner Gunn's ideological approach to *Walden*, a major monument in American letters but a difficult work to locate within autobiography. She succeeds admirably, I think, in showing the limitations of certain contemporary critics and philosophers who would confine autobiography either to "the self writing" (discourse) or "the self written" (history). Either way, she argues, autobiography becomes no more than the artistic effort to rescue the self from time's flux and fix it in words forever. These superficial assumptions (seen in the work of Mutlu Konik Blasing, Louis Renza, and Jeffrey Mehlman) arbitrarily confine autobiography to literary art. By stressing *Walden* as a fully cultural act of *reading* the self's reflections in the eye of the world and then *speaking* one's fullest temporality, Gunn asserts the vital links between spiritual testament and autobiography, and thus between religious hermeneutics and autobiographical criticism.

Regarded simply as literature, autobiography is indeed a problematic mode of discourse. The fact that "genre" is a term critics use gingerly nowadays highlights the dangers of too-specific definitions. Darrel Mansell's essay examines and explodes attempts to separate fact from fiction, science from art, historical record from imaginative creation, truth from beauty or pleasure. These are all false distinctions. A truer description of autobiography is contained in Jean Starobinski's term *discourse-history*. The autobiographer aims to re-create the self-in-its-world, not by literal reproduction of remembered facts (a boring as well as impossible achievement), but by patterning the past into a present symbolic truth. If the differences between literal and symbolic truths are dubious to some writers (witness the games played in the name of autobiography by surfictionists like Ron Sukenick or Frederick Exley), they are usually clearer for the common reader. Mansell agrees with Norman N. Holland that any piece of autobiographical prose can be taken as either fact or fiction. Yet our expectations depend heavily upon all sorts of obvious clues to authorial intention such as a preface, photographs, even cover blurbs or library classifications. Using such cues, the reader completes the autobiographical act in much the same way the psychoanalyst's interpretation completes a dream. Mansell's argument is echoed by others, including Barrett John Mandel and

Philippe Lejeune, who point out that writers and readers form a "pact" or contractual community. They commonly agree that the language of autobiography points both *outward* to the world of remembered experience and *inward* to a reflective consciousness. Thus like all narratives—including, of course, histories—autobiography is simultaneously fiction and fact.

Most of the essayists represented here, therefore, take a cultural rather than a narrowly literary tack in dealing with autobiography. They devote surprisingly small space to matters of mode or genre: e.g., memoir, confession, apology, reminiscence, journal, diary. This derives from the widespread agreement that autobiography is best understood as a content, not a form. Older critics like Roy Pascal once insisted upon testing for the "true autobiography," but this purist criticism has now given way to more inclusive expectations and looser definitions. Nonetheless, memory and the retrospective stance are still widely held to be essential sources of the truths personal history affords. These hallowed Diltheyan assumptions are, however, directly challenged by Anaïs Nin. For this unique yet surprisingly representative artist, psychoanalyst, immigrant, and feminist, the autobiographical enterprise achieves unexpected depths in the diary. Her passionate argument is that memory actually obscures the shape of the self by setting up false categories. As immediate art, everyday self-therapy, and running social record, the diary derives its accuracy from its secrecy or privacy. It is a place even more accessible than Walden Pond where one can go in order to discover a self. Especially for women (as Suzanne Juhasz also asserts), the instantaneous self-portrait is truer than more formal modes of self-re-creation. These are often linked to conventional social roles and career considerations, and to particular stages of the life cycle. As her own *Diary* illustrates in the later volumes, the diary need not be fragmentary, domestic, narcissistic; it can open out on the rest of the world. But in order to play one's part in that larger world, Nin argues, one must first *exist*. Personal identity, she reminds us, is an achievement, never an inevitability. The diary can be a vehicle for waking up to life permanently. It is, moreover, in several other respects a model for all autobiography: since it does not depend upon publication, it is available to everyone, not just the talented or famous; it is wedded to no particular form and so can take its imprint from experience directly.

Journals and diaries are ways of discovering one's depth. They can prove the paradox that "the personal life, deeply lived, takes you beyond the personal."

Anaïs Nin's *Diary* does not, of course, conform to the usual pattern of the private journal. Its indefatigable author and Gunther Stuhlmann edited it later for publication, thus imposing upon a periodic record of events and emotions the retrospective consciousness of conventional autobiography. Nevertheless, her narrative stands near one end of the spectrum of autobiographical options. It is supremely an individual story which resists easy ideological translation. "There is not one big cosmic meaning for all," she declares in *Diary I*, "there is only the meaning we each give to our life, an individual meaning, an individual plot, like an individual novel, a book for each person. To seek a total unity is wrong" (p. vii). At the other end of the spectrum are works like *Soledad Brother* which seem to owe their existence to an ideological impulse which almost automatically provides a context and handle for the life-story. These are narratives in which the self is self-consciously submerged. American autobiography offers an almost infinite variety of narratives strung out along this spectrum. Because each autobiography is a cultural artifact celebrating individual consciousness, style, and experience, its readers must learn to adjust critical focus from *individual text* to *social context* to *appropriate conceptual frameworks*—and, I would argue, *back to the single text again.* For we are chiefly interested in autobiographies in order to find out how people, events, things, institutions, ideas, emotions, relationships have become meaningful to a single mind as it uses language to pattern the past. As critics of culture, therefore, our task resembles that of the oral historian or the anthropologist. Ronald Grele speaks for the oral historian: "Our aim is to bring to conscious articulation the ideological problematic of the author, to reveal the cultural context in which information is being conveyed, and to transform an individual story into a cultural narrative, and so to understand more fully what happened in the past." * Such an objective, we note, runs counter as well as parallel to Anaïs Nin's individuating impulse. Autobiography inevitably involves such tensions and contradictions. Because its object is stubbornly multi-

---

*"Movement without Aim: Methodological and Theoretical Problems in Oral History," in *Envelopes of Sound. Six Practitioners Discuss the Method, Theory, and Practice of Oral History and Oral Testimony* (Chicago: Precedent Pub., 1975), p. 142.

dimensional, the study of autobiography is a participant-observer science or art, like anthropology. Each author stands both within and outside individual experience, for each is in effect an anthropologist returned from a sojourn in the country of his or her own past. Readers, too, are travellers and interviewers. Each of us is co-creator of another's story. Since each account is a thickly dimensional original act, each must be assessed differently, though always with an eye for similarities. Michael Agar, an urban anthropologist who collects the life-stories of bums and drug addicts, suggests a way of reconciling the methodological tensions between Ronald Grele and Anaïs Nin. "Complex forms are approached recognizing the simultaneous relevance of several different kinds of explanatory schemata," he writes. "The form is untangled to facilitate analysis, and then retangled to learn what has been gained in understanding the original complex form" (p. 234).

The following essays and bibliography, then, offer guidelines, models, and demonstrations toward the untangling and retangling of American autobiographies.

The Proper Study: Autobiographies in American Studies

by Robert F. Sayre

Autobiographies, in all their bewildering number and variety, offer the student in American Studies a broader and more direct contact with American experience than any other kind of writing. For they have been written in almost every part of the country by presidents and thieves, judges and professors, Indians and immigrants (of nearly every nationality), by ex-slaves and slaveowners, by men and women in practically every line of work, abolitionists to zookeepers, by adolescents and octogenarians, counterfeiters, captives, muggers, muckrakers, preachers, and everybody else. The catalogue is as great as one of Walt Whitman's own...or greater. It is the true Song of Myself. And Ourselves.

The bibliographies listed at the end of this volume are a partial verification. Louis Kaplan's *Bibliography of American Autobiographies* lists 6,377 titles, and it covers only works published before 1945, the year in which he and his associates began to assemble them. Its forty-five-page subject index also breaks the entries down according to occupations, regions, and (where applicable) the foreign countries from which the writers came or in which they later lived. The defects in the book are that its subject descriptions are often vague and that it excludes several kinds of writing about which many people might be most curious: slave narratives; Indian captivity narratives; travel, sporting, and adventure narratives "in which the autobiographical element is insignificant"; and journals, diaries, and collections of letters. Some of these defects are made up by Russell C. Brignano's

"The Proper Study: Autobiographies in American Studies" by Robert F. Sayre. Slightly abridged from *American Quarterly*, 29, no. 3 (Bibliographical Issue 1977), 241-58. Copyright 1977, Trustees of the University of Pennsylvania. Reprinted by permission of the author and the University of Pennsylvania.

Black America in Autobiography and will be further remedied by the works of Mary Louise Briscoe, Patricia Addis, Delores K. Gros-Louis, and Carolyn Rhodes. Richard G. Lillard's *American Life in Autobiography* is a selection of 400 books which Lillard read and summarized in a paragraph each. However, it mainly covers works printed or reprinted since 1900, listing them according to the authors' occupations. Thus, there is still a need for annotated bibliographies of earlier American autobiographies.

Yet until quite recently, autobiographies have not received very much scholarly attention. The English departments of the 1950s and early '60s generally scorned them as an inferior kind of literature. They were not works of imagination, not *belles lettres*. They did not seem to demand the ingenious analysis of structure, theme, image, and myth which one devoted to a Donne poem or a Faulkner novel. To say that a novel was "autobiographical" was to show knowing disapproval. *Redburn* and *This Side of Paradise* were autobiographical; *Moby-Dick* and *The Great Gatsby* were art. History departments, meanwhile, believed that autobiographies were too subjective. As the author's own account of his life and work, an autobiography was sure to be biased and one-sided. A serious historian or biographer was duty-bound to correct such incomplete accounts of things. As a result, a student in American Studies, getting most of his teaching from professors of English and history, was not likely to hear many good words about autobiographies. They were attacked from both sides, bastards whom neither parent would defend.

Ironically, the American Studies student has or had a similar curse. He has sought his own legitimacy by getting literature and history to marry, and autobiographies already represent an indissoluble common-law marriage. They are history in that they are source materials, containing facts and interpreting facts, preserving the past, and drawing lessons from it. They are literature in that they must please and entertain as well as teach. And like both history and literature, they have to select and narrate. They have to organize their materials, address an audience, and, in more subtle ways, create audiences, find links between the actor-writers who are in them and the readers, then or generations later, who are outside and must be engaged, drawn in. To legitimate himself, the student of American culture might seek to understand these other literary-historical crossbreeds.

The oldest and in some respects still most fundamental theoretician of autobiography was the nineteenth-century German philosopher of history, Wilhelm Dilthey. Regrettably, only a fraction of his work has been translated, but the selections made by H. P. Rickman in *Pattern and Meaning in History* show that understanding of the individual, through the individual's own understanding of himself and his time, in autobiography, was at the center of Dilthey's conception of history. To Dilthey there were no Zeitgeists, philosophical essences, or other monolithic interpretations of history. For him "there was no one'meaning of life,'" Rickman says, "but only the meaning which individuals perceived in, or attributed to their own lives." So the autobiographer or, in Dilthey's words, the "person who seeks the connecting threads in the history of his life" is the primary historian, and the later historian seeking meanings as another age knew them should begin with autobiographers. They tell us what life was, as they conceived it and organized it in their living and as they then put it into retrospective language.

Dilthey's few paragraphs on Augustine, Rousseau, and Goethe are too brief for one to tell what his own methods of analysis might have been, but his ideas lay behind his student Georg Misch's *History of Autobiography in Antiquity*. Misch's book is dull Germanic scholarship, but it is important in at least two ways. It shows that there was no "autobiography," in a modern sense, until St. Augustine. (The very word was not coined until the early nineteenth century.) But it also shows that personal expressions of the meaning of life, in Dilthey's sense, certainly did exist and that a study of them, in whatever forms they took, is rewarding. Indeed the forms and conventions are as interesting as the content. They reveal the relationships of the writer or speaker to his culture, how the individual could speak about himself.

Misch's work, therefore, might persuade students of American autobiography to make their definitions broad enough to take in all forms of self-history. Yet definition is difficult, and controversial. Most people who wrote about autobiography in the last ten or twenty years (including the present writer) adopted definitions more or less like those of Georges Gusdorf and Roy Pascal. Autobiography, said Pascal, "involves the reconstruction of the movement of a life, or part of a life, in the actual circumstances in which it was lived ... It imposes a pattern on a life, constructs out of it a coherent story. It establishes certain stages in an individual life, makes links between them, and defines, implicitly or explicitly, a certain consistency of relation-

ship between the self and the outside world..." Pascal considered letters and diaries to be autobiographical but not autobiography, because they did not have a single point of view and were not written
from a single point in time. Memoirs were too external, self-portraits
too static, and autobiographical fiction was also generally excluded
from pure autobiography because the author had license, whether he
took it or not, to change and invent. Thus the major precursor of
modern autobiography, according to this definition, was the religious
conversion narrative. Its authors looked back from a single, organizing perspective and told a fairly coherent story of a sizeable portion
of their lives. John Morris' *Versions of the Self: Studies in English Autobiography from John Bunyan to John Stuart Mill* is a very instructive
history of this tradition of autobiography and of its contributions to
modern literature and modern concepts of the self.

Yet recent books and articles have had trouble with this definition
and, along with it, the related standards of evaluation. In *Metaphors
of Self,* James Olney begins by making some Jungian refinements of it
—distinguishing between autobiographies "simplex" which tell the
one story of a career, conversion, or achievement and the autobiographies "duplex" which attempt to portray a whole person. But
Olney's last chapter on Eliot's *Four Quartets* stretches the definition
to the breaking point. If the *Four Quartets* are autobiography, what
isn't? If it is legitimate to include Eliot as an autobiographer, aren't
there many other authors who should be included too, by making the
definition less restrictive? Previously, in "Autobiography as Narrative," Alfred Kazin had implied a broader definition in saying that
"autobiography, like other literary forms, is what a gifted writer
makes of it." Kazin was most interested in the large number of modern
books like Hemingway's *A Moveable Feast* and Robert Lowell's *Life
Studies* which use fictional techniques yet "deliberately retain the
facts behind the story in order to show the imaginative possibilities
inherent in fact." That kind of writing, which, as Kazin said, is "very
characteristic of our period," is hard to approach as traditional autobiography. It doesn't tell the same kind of story; its chronology is
likely to be fragmentary or shuffled, inventive and exploratory; it
approaches fiction.

Barrett John Mandel, however, was disturbed by Kazin's implications that autobiography could take such liberties and should
therefore be judged according to the supposedly higher aesthetic
standards of fiction. In "The Autobiographer's Art" he insisted on

the reader's right to know whether he was reading fiction or fact and the autobiographer's right to be judged as an autobiographer and not a novelist. Francis Hart, as another participant in this debate, attempted to find his answers in the actual practice of some forty autobiographers since Rousseau. Scholarly and theoretical answers to the questions of the interplay of fiction and history, form, and authorial intention were, Hart said, "prescriptive" and "premature."

The debate over definitions arose in yet another way when Richard Gilman, reviewing Eldridge Cleaver's *Soul on Ice*, wrote "that white critics have not the right to make judgments on a certain kind of black writing." Cleaver, Malcolm X, and other angry black writers wrote with an immediacy and sense of purpose and mission which white critics, accustomed to *The Education of Henry Adams* or Newman's *Apologia*. could not appreciate. Reading Gilman's reviews, republished in *The Confusion of Realms*, brings back the raging arguments of the 1960s when his position was taken, for varying reasons, by both black and white, activist and conservative. But Gilman was answered convincingly by Warner Berthoff. Writing mainly about *The Autobiography of Malcolm X* and Norman Mailer's *The Armies of the Night*. Berthoff argued that critics did have a responsibility to assess this literature of "Witness and Testament" and to recognize its precedents in autobiographical traditions. "The open letter, the preachment, the apology, the parable or representative anecdote, the capitulatory brief, the tirade, the narrative or polemical exposé, the public prayer, the appeal to conscience, the call to arms" was Berthoff's list of the genres which Cleaver and other black writers had used. Not to recognize these as sometimes the most important forms of autobiography would be like throwing away half the tools (and weapons) of survival.

To add my own testimony and tabulations to the question, I can only say that in the last fifteen years or so I have read about 400 American autobiographies (very broadly defined), and that they have been like a private history, in several senses, of the amazing crimes, achievements, banalities, and wonders of American life. Orthodox history is, by contrast, a bland soup. This history is unorthodox, heterodox. For example, take the impostor's tale. This is a story where the author either is or has been an impostor, or where his tale is so improbable that he has been charged with being one and must tell the tale to authenticate himself. The rogues' biographies and autobiographical fictions and non-fictions of Defoe and Fielding were the immediate European predecessors, and Ebenezer Cooke's pre-Barthian *Sot-Weed Factor* was an early American approach to it. But *The Memoirs of the Notorious Stephen Burroughs of New Hampshire* is the masterpiece. Burroughs, who flourished between about 1780 and 1810, was an impostor-clergyman (he stole his uncle's sermons), a counterfeiter (he decided that he believed in a large money supply), a schoolteacher on Long Island, and later a salesman of western lands. His book was apparently very popular in the early 1800s, but was almost forgotten until Robert Frost persuaded the Dial Press to republish it in 1924. It is a stunning revelation of American gullibility and sure-enough social mobility.

An even more remarkable case is John Dunn Hunter, author of *Memoirs of Captivity among the Indians of North America* (1824). Hunter was called an impostor because his tale of having been captured as an infant and raised among the Kansas and Osage tribes simply seemed incredible — and because his pro-Indian attitudes challenged government policy. Richard Drinnon has recently vindicated Hunter in the biography *White Savage*, but the charge that he was an impostor prevented his influencing the policies he attacked.

The sagas of Burroughs and Hunter also suggest that in those ages before transcripts, identity cards, and rapid communication, impostors were indeed more frequent. The ones in *Huckleberry Finn* and *The Confidence Man* were not mere inventions. But perhaps Americans were also less sure of each other because they were so profoundly unsure of themselves. At one moment they bragged like fighting cocks; at another they were dour and insecure. An impostor with confidence and determination could escape with a lot, as William and Ellen Craft did in *Running a Thousand Miles for Freedom*. By Ellen's dressing as a white master and William's pretending to be "his"/her body servant, these slaves escaped with their lives. Yet we shouldn't be too sure that such escapades are over. The falsified lives of Chief Red Fox and Howard Hughes and the purportedly true underground lives of Abbie Hoffman and Patricia Hearst are ample proof that lies are still told and truth still uncertain.

Susan Kuhlmann's *Knave, Fool, and Genius* is among the several studies of the fictional confidence man in America. But no book, to my knowledge, has investigated his autobiographical and biographical real-life origins (or replicas) in books like Burroughs' *Memoirs* and *Ringolevio: A Life Played for Keeps*, by Emmet Grogan. Grogan, legendary founder of the Diggers in San Francisco in the 1960s, resembles Burroughs in some ways. You never know whether he is lying and putting you on or not. Thus one further value in studying these books is that they make the sometimes nit-picking aesthetic questions of "pose" and persona a life-and-death matter. Is Grogan right that only thieves and revolutionaries play for keeps? Does the artist and "straight" merely play for fun?

Another subject for study is the secret diary, which has immense contemporary significance because of the Nixon tapes. Diaries, we have assumed, are only source material for biographers and historians. We think that they are not literature because diarists cannot fully anticipate and arrange the events they record and because they are supposedly only talking to themselves. But these problems never reduced the interest which we find in some great ones like Samuel Sewall's, those of the Adams family, George Templeton Strong's, and Thoreau's *Journal*. Privacy—a person's right to keep and record things to himself—has encouraged some people to write as they otherwise could not. Secrecy, too, may be necessary when the thoughts or facts are about other people and could damage them, the recorder, and still larger groups. But both privacy and secrecy are relative. William Byrd's *Secret History of the Dividing Line* was not for publication but was apparently read to Byrd's friends. *The Journal of Charlotte L. Forten* was private primarily because Charlotte, as a wealthy black Philadelphian, had no friendly listeners to whom she could express her sense of frustration and isolation. White girls at pre-Civil War New England academies were often required to keep diaries and also required to show them to their teachers! Anaïs Nin's diaries became destined for publication; as Robert Fothergill shows in *Private Chronicles*, they became the fulfillment of her literary ambitions. James J. Fahey's *Pacific War Diary*, not published until 1963, had to be secret because naval regulations forbade it and because the things he wrote about some officers might have gotten him in trouble. Yet he kept it devotedly, despite his utter exhaustion after long hours at battle stations, and it is one of the most vivid accounts of World War II which I have read. There are other diaries and letters from every war, and one suspects that they may still be "secret," in the sense of forgotten or suppressed, because we still do not think of war from the ordinary soldier's or sailor's viewpoint. (The modern Russian scholars of American literature, by contrast, show great interest in such a work as

Philip Freneau's "Prison Ship," and one wishes to hear more of their reasons.[1]) When we say a prison diary or war diary is merely boring or illiterate, repetitious and inconsequential, we need to ask ourselves what we really mean, and why we say it. For these can be the words of consciousness suppressing bad dreams and the unwanted messages of history and the unconscious. We need no more dramatic evidence of the efforts to which a supposedly rational and governing consciousness will go in such suppression—and the tireless energy necessary to dig out the truth—than the stories of White House tapes and *All the President's Men*. We may guard the "tapes" to our own personal and collective transgressions just as fiercely as Nixon "stonewalled" his critics.

The whole matter of secrecy in diaries and autobiographies obviously needs discussion. Bruce Mazlish's "Autobiography and Psycho-analysis—Between Truth and Self-Deception" does an inadequate job of showing how modern autobiography has been influenced by Freudian theory. Jeffrey Mehlman's *A Structural Study of Autobiography* concentrates too much, for the American reader, on French autobiographers. Moreover, Mehlman's implications that because he is following questions in the later works of Freud he is therefore more serious than other scholars is cult nonsense, a mixture of vanity and exclusiveness. But his initial questions are basic. How does one become "alive *(bio)* to oneself *(auto)* in the exclusive realm that the French call *écriture (graphie)*"?

But the issue of secrecy is just one part of the overall question of what autobiography *reveals*. However secret or open, what can be learned from it which cannot be so readily learned from drama, fiction, history, and other forms of expression? Or to put the question pedagogically, what does it teach? The existence and planning of many courses in American autobiography, taught in both American Studies and English departments, makes the question very pertinent. What are the organizing themes in its history?

For thoughtful answers we may turn to Karl J. Weintraub's essay on "Autobiography and Historical Consciousness." Like Dilthey, Weintraub is interested in autobiography's "very special function in elucidating history." And the greatest value in autobiography, he feels, is in the basic conceptions of self and personality which it

---

[1]A.N. Nikolyukin, "Past and Present Discussions of American National Literature," *New Literary History*, (1973), 575-90.

reveals. People have written different kinds of autobiography in different times and cultures because of their different self-conceptions. He also hastens to insist that "one can study self-conception without having to be a Freudian, Jungian, Skinnerian, or what have we," for the point is to realize how an autobiographer conceived of his own life and not just what one discipline of psychologists or economists would perceive in it. Self-conceptions have a history and a full humanistic range of interest, and while they can be read most intensely in the history of autobiography, that reading must be further informed by as much additional historical knowledge and insight as the reader possesses. The latter part of Weintraub's essay is a short but brilliantly illustrated outline of such autobiographical self-conceptions from classical antiquity to the nineteenth century.

Some other readers, I realize, might prefer to organize their study along more specifically ideological lines. One could after all read autobiographies as a Marxist, an Eriksonian, or with great interest as an historian of ethnic and sexual oppression and liberation. But the greater advantage in Weintraub's approach is that it encourages a wider view, without necessarily excluding these others. It therefore has considerable suggestiveness to students in American Studies, most of whom would like to use such particular ideologies or disciplines and at the same time not be constricted by them. But be that as it may, I have found Weintraub's relation of the history of autobiography to the history of concepts of self to be so useful that I would like to follow it. It suggests what might yet be done with American autobiography, while still allowing one to talk about what has been done in recent (and not so recent) scholarship and criticism. My only modification will be to accept a broader definition of autobiography than his. Instead of saying "*that form* in which an author undertakes a retrospective vision over a significant portion of his life, perceiving his life as a process of interaction with a coexistent world," I would like to say "*those forms...*" As should already be clear, I don't think we can have an adequate history of American autobiography which is not as plural in genre as it is pluralistic in subject matter. When there is so much to say and so little space, being so inclusive may be all the more presumptuous. But we cannot talk about concepts of self (and selves) without realizing that the concepts inevitably take different literary forms as well as different social and cultural ones.

This history begins, obviously, with the Indians. And a course in autobiography is perhaps better prepared to deal with this fact than most others, even though the recording of Indian "autobiographies" did not begin until the nineteenth century and writing by Indians themselves until the twentieth century. But Lynne Woods O'Brien's pamphlet, _Plains Indian Autobiographies_, shows that Native Americans clearly did have their own forms of autobiography such as coup stories and visions (which still exist in pictographs) and the stories later recorded by white collectors developed from them. L. L. Langness' _The Life History in Anthropological Science_ has a long bibliography of the dictated autobiographies and a professional discussion of the collectors' methods. So Indian autobiography clearly can be taught in American Studies classes and makes more than just a "token." It reveals, for one thing, a set of self-conceptions in which, as in _Black Elk Speaks_, self-history is impossible to separate from tribal welfare and a collective conscious and unconscious life.

Yet the Puritans also had a sense of their lives unfolding within a grand cosmic drama, and this has long made the study of autobiographies one of the most rewarding approaches to them. Perry Miller's books and essays on the New England mind are, in a way, an extended treatment of Puritan self-history. Sacvan Berkovitch's _Puritan Origins of the American Self_, which moves beyond Miller's intellectual history to a complex study of Puritan typology, promises to be a successor to Miller's work in both its density and, unfortunately, its obscurity. The chapters on personal narratives in Kenneth Murdock's _Literature and Theology in Colonial New England_ are still a more available and pleasing introduction. Daniel Shea criticizes both Miller and Murdock, however, for limiting their studies of autobiography to conversion narratives and the not very typical autobiography of Thomas Shepard. The conversion narrative, Shea shows, was such a fixed form that one reads pretty much like another. Not even Edward Taylor could depart from it and tell a recognizably individual story. Shea's comprehensive reading of both the conventional and the unconventional early American spiritual autobiographies makes his book currently the best. It has excellent chapters on the Quakers and John Woolman, on the Mathers, and on Jonathan Edwards.

The early American concept of self may emerge most clearly, however, in the narratives of Indian captivity. There the writer's or scribe's sense of being a white Christian European is in bold relief against the supposed horrors and temptations of the wilderness and another culture. Only recently have we begun to realize their importance. In the late 1940s and early '50s, Roy Harvey Pearce treated them as a sub-literary genre whose interest was in their prejudices about Indians and their contributions to the themes and situations of later fiction. Richard Slotkin has shown that their significance is greater, because their prejudices and archetypes have been more influential. James Axtell, on the other hand, has used them for what they can be relied upon to tell about Indian life and to explain why so many captives preferred Indian life to white. Richard Vanderbeets attributes their popularity to their ritualistic patterns of a person's "Separation, Transformation, and Return."

That Benjamin Franklin secularized spiritual autobiography is a familiar point, but the result is not the smug and artless little guide to riches which the Wanamakers cherished and D. H. Lawrence loathed. Franklin, as John William Ward showed in "Who Was Benjamin Franklin?," artfully used the *Autobiography* to compose himself. In *The Interpreted Design*, David L.Minter has gone on to examine the narrative techniques of Franklin the writer. John Lynen's *Design of the Present* also has a very good chapter on Franklin's relation to his own past and its meaning. Opposing views of the *Autobiography's* contribution to the success myth are in John Cawelti's *Apostles of the Self-Made Man* and William Spengemann's and L. R. Lundquist's "Autobiography and the American Myth." But we also can't forget that the *Autobiography* was addressed to Franklin's son, and Claude-Anne Lopez's and Eugenia W. Herbert's biography, *The Private Franklin*, is of special interest because it studies him in his role as father and famous relative to dozens of dependent siblings, nephews, and nieces. Lopez and Herbert bring out Franklin the bourgeois family man, who tried to aid and promote his relatives but also had to recognize their limitations. Their book illustrates the advantages of biography as a supplement to autobiography.

In the early nineteenth century, autobiography united the struggle to develop an indigenous literature with the even more fundamental motive to define and create an American character. The tacit second question after Crèvecoeur's "What then is an American?" is, "And who am I?" It was asked in a book which represented several autobiographical forms—the epistle, the travel narrative, and the idealizing pastoral ecologue, all of which were common in the early national literature. Epistolary forms, both signed and pseudonymous, personal and political, were common in the pamphlets and literature of controversy. Travel books, in which the writer had the opportunity to define himself as an American against the backgrounds of Europe, the sea, and the American West, were continued by Dana, Irving, Margaret Fuller, Parkman, and many later writers, famous and obscure.

It was in the 1840s and '50s, however, that American autobiographical writing became most diverse and original. The most uniquely American, we now see, was the slave narrative, created *sui generis* by the conditions of a racially and politically divided country. Where the convention of many later white autobiographies was the success story, the convention of the slave narrative was the escape from bondage to freedom, or a degree of it. This looked back, in some ways, to the pattern of early Pilgrim and settler literature. It also looked forward to later black autobiography, as Gilbert Osofsky, Stephen Butterfield, Sidonie Smith, and many others have said. Butterfield, in addition, makes a very strong case for black autobiography as the "heart of autobiography in American literature," because personal experience there so closely unites history and art. But the autobiographies of any oppressed people make conceptions of self peculiarly important. A necessary step in anyone's liberation from stereotypes and injustice is the moment when he or she asserts his or her own rights and values against those imposed from without. This *is* the discovery of self, and it is what has made autobiography such an important ideological weapon, not only in the abolitionist era but in the civil rights era, and to many other groups and causes. James Olney's *Tell Me Africa*, though not about American autobiography at all, still shows vital recognition of this in his opening chapters on the value of autobiography to an American trying to understand modern African artists and political leaders. Moreover, as Albert E. Stone says in his essay on Frederick Douglass's *Narrative*, the ex-slave (or ex-colonial, we can add) turned to autobiography because he wished to make his story an example to other people and a justification of his continued fight. He had urgent answers to the question any autobiographer is asked, "Why am I writing the story of my life?" Scratch the surface of an American autobiography, James Cox noted in his essay on Franklin, Thoreau, Whitman, and Henry Adams, and somewhere inside is a revolution or a revolutionary.

The self-assertive white writers of the American Renaissance are, nevertheless, a somewhat more difficult group to place in an autobiographical framework than their black contemporaries. They cannot be left out, because their philosophic sympathies were so strong, approaching exhortation. Where was the American Dante, demanded Emerson, who would "write his autobiography into colossal cipher, or into universality"? But their practices were so idiosyncratic and diverse, ranging from Hawthorne's guarded but profoundly revealing auto-bibli-ography to *The Scarlet Letter* to Whitman's brash but profoundly shifty and anonymous *Song of Myself.* One can agree with Lawrence Buell in *Literary Transcendentalism* that "the most egotistical movement in American literary history produced no first-rate autobiography, unless one counts *Walden* as such." The reasons, Buell feels, are that the Transcendentalists (and the same could probably be said of Hawthorne and Melville) had both historical and personal reasons for making a paradox of their self-preoccupation and their desire for self-transcendence. Their democratic, romantic, and Protestant values all demanded self-examination but also proscribed it and redirected it towards universals. Democracy, as Tocqueville perceived, restricted freedom of opinion and made Americans fond of general ideas. Romantic thought in America turned even more to nature than it had in England and France. Protestant spritual autobiography became "more complex, more literary, and less intimate."

On the other hand, we could invert Buell's evidence and say that these same influences actually provoked Emerson, Thoreau, Whitman, and Melville into expansions and improvements on autobiographical forms rather than evasions of them. The old forms were inadequate, as might be proved by a closer examination of the botches made by such contemporaries as Orestes Brownson. Margaret Fuller, as Bell Gale Chevigny shows in her collection of Fuller's writing and the writing about her, was a person whose need for liberated self-conceptions in both literature and life was tragically intense. But finding new literary metaphors of the self required the greatest American audacity. When they began writing, none of the major writers of the American Renaissance, with the possible exception of Melville, had met one of the major requirements of autobiography: they hadn't done anything. Spiritual autobiographies had been open to the less famous because they emphasized what had *happened to* the writer more than what he had achieved. But Rousseau and Franklin and an increasingly broad, secular society had reduced the importance of narrowly religious histories. A great autobiography had to come from a great man like Franklin or an infamous egotist like Rousseau (a figure most Americans then despised). In England similar restrictions made Wordsworth and Mill refrain from publishing

their masterpieces, while Carlyle went through his charade with a
tailor. So when Whitman published his *Leaves of Grass* in 1855, it
contained very little that can be called "personal experience." It was
a vicarious national autobiography, with democratic general ideas
and long lists of everybody's business. Thoreau, meanwhile, had
found his outlet by doing something so cranky, going out to *be* instead
of *do*, that an accounting was justified. Melville, having fitted his
earlier experiences into the formulas of captivity narratives and sea
stories, eventually universalized his autobiography also. The self was
at once a daring cosmic revolutionary and a pantheistical and calm
solitary observer.

The Civil War seems to have brought a return to more traditional
forms of autobiography, just as it reawakened some of the other ghosts
of old Calvinist righteousness and later a business conservatism. Like
all wars, it was an occasion for military memoirs (not to bury Caesar
but to revive him); of these, Grant's is a classic. In its modesty and
firm resolution, its realistic language and ever-increasing epic range,
it is a great monument of both Grant the man and the armies he led.
Two other classics of the Civil War are John William de Forest's
partially autobiographical novel *Miss Ravenel's Conversion from Seces-
sion to Loyalty* and Whitman's hospital notes in *Specimen Days*. From
the Southern side, the greatest work is Mary Boykin Chesnut's *Diary
from Dixie*. Yet with the exception of Edmund Wilson's absorbing
chapters in *Patriotic Gore*, which examines these and other works
mainly for their documentary value, very little has been written
about them as autobiographical literature. They are, to be sure, military memoirs, novel, journal, and diary. They are not within the
narrow limits of what Gusdorf called "*autobiographie proprement dite.*"
But this only indicates again that the definition is what may be wrong.
We need to ask why writers chose these genres as proper, as their own.

In contrast to this neglect of Civil War autobiography is the enormous current interest in Henry Adams. He is mentioned in nearly
every book and article on American autobiography as a whole and
studied in detail in many other places. But as I look at him and his
associates and contemporaries in this rapid and yet long-range historical perspective, what is most striking is a new conception of the
self as defined not by nature or religion or specific events and
achievements but by family, history, and civilization. He resembles
Gibbon in this respect, but Gibbon in America, where civilization
had simultaneously just triumphed and just become terrifying, a

machine, a dynamo of vast and uncertain potential. James, Howells, and even Mark Twain give the same sense in their autobiographies of being proudly civilized men of the world who had travelled and seen great change, but their responses are different from his. To a greater degree than Adams, they looked backward, enveloped themselves in the lyrical joys of childhood. They were closer than Adams to the explicitly nostalgic autobiographies of the late nineteenth century—Lucy Larcom's *A New England Girlhood*, Edward Everett Hale's *A New England Boyhood*, and Charles Eastman's *Indian Boyhood*. Yet these too illustrate the coming of an adulthood which was vastly enlarged and chaotic. Adulthood was so different, it required a second book. Eastman's second life—perhaps the most altered one of all—was in *From the Deep Woods to Civilization*. James' later reflections are in *The American Scene*. And Mark Twain, sometimes recoiling from his civilized world as desperately as Adams, gave up altogether on a unified autobiography. As Jay Martin has suggested in *Harvests of Change*, Mark Twain's consequent experiments in autobiography look ahead to Gertrude Stein and Conrad Aiken.

What I am rather hastily and tentatively suggesting is that from about 1900 onwards the concept of self in America is very closely related to the concept of civilization and that the forms and structures of autobiography reflect this, inevitably also reflecting different personal and generational responses to the promises and perils of modern civilization. For the writers of Adams's generation wrote what Thomas Cooley has suggestively called *Educated Lives*. Education, in both the formal and the larger senses, plays an enormous part in these lives. Education, in Adams' many senses, became the necessary preparation for a new civilization, the only possible means of regaining control over it, and so also the unifying (or dis-unifying?) theme of autobiography. The identity of modern man was in his relation to the rewards and demands, hopes and horrors of the complex civilized society in which he lived. Travel, religion, nature, and even personal success in this society had ceased to be individually important; they had been swallowed up in it. We can outline modern responses to this civilized multiverse, as Adams called it, by looking briefly at three generations of twentieth century autobiographers. Those in the first generation, on the whole, were journalists, progressives, and professionals. They were born in the 1860s and '70s and reached the active period of their careers between about 1895 and 1920: Edith Wharton, Jane Addams, Teddy Roosevelt, Lincoln Steffens, Frederic C. Howe, S. S. McClure, Charlotte Perkins Gilman, Ray Stannard Baker, Ida Tarbell, Upton Sinclair, Hamlin Garland, Richard Ely, William Allen White, Booker T. Washington, Jacob Riis, Edward Bok, Mabel Dodge Luhan, Louis Sullivan, the Hapgoods, Tom Johnson, Clarence Darrow. Some were aristocrats, some prairie farmers; some became socialists, some solid Republicans. Yet in the form of their autobiographies, they are astonishingly alike. Many came from small towns in western Pennsyvania or the Middle West, a few from mansions in California and New York, but the latter part of their lives were *in* the new industrial civilization—writing for newspapers, travelling on Pullman trains and ocean liners, lecturing, organizing, and vacationing in some summer cottage or cabin. All these activities were a function of their work, their jobs. (Thus they justify the assumption behind Richard Lillard's *American Life in Autobiography* that classifications of autobiography should be made according to careers or professions.) But careers became important because the new industrial civilization offered such a variety of interesting ones. It also had such a variety of problems on which critics and reformers could work—monopolies, immigration, the shame of the cities, modern marriage, the color line, and so on. Understandably, a great deal of history has since been written about their work, their origins, points of view, and motives. But they have not been studied very much as autobiographers. Milan James Kedro's "Autobiography as a Key to Identity of the Progressive Era" and Robert Stinson's "S. S. McClure's *My Autobiography*; The Progressive as Self-Made Man" are the best essays on them which I know. Christopher Lasch's *The New Radicalism in America*, though not specifically about their autobiographies, is very incisive about their personalities and self-images. But their similar autobiographies are an amazing picture of their collective identity. They wrote the first large group of American autobiographies to be entitled *The Autobiography of...*, and the definition was simply a biography written by one's self. The books usually cover the full range from youth to middle or old age, and they self-consciously stand in their firm, big bindings as monuments to the life and work of the author. Thus, despite these authors' many criticisms of their society, their books still reveal their thorough involvement in it. The building of new institutions, the reform of old ones, and the realizing of new careers had absorbed the writers' life long energies and enthusiasms.

The next generation, which came of age in the 1920s and '30s, had a much more serious quarrel with the civilization into which they were born. Gertrude Stein's name for it, the Lost Generation, still holds, for its leaders were not people who found meaningful work in causes and professions; they were writers and artists who rebelled. Yet even their rebellion had uncertain direction. Thus these auto-biographers—Eugene O'Neill, Sinclair Lewis, Sherwood Anderson, Conrad Aiken, Dos Passos, Hemingway, Fitzgerald, James T. Farrell, Gertrude Stein, Hart Crane, Hilda Doolittle, Edmund Wilson, E. E. Cummings, Henry Roth, Thomas Wolfe—chose much less tradi-tional, discreet, and clearly organized forms. Their most traditional genre, perhaps, was the *Bildungsroman*, which not only described their anguished coming of age, in small towns or Eastern colleges, but also gave the child's vision of the sickness and terror of the adult world. Another revealing genre was the autobiographical war novel. In it, civilization was E. E. Cummings' foul French prison or Hemingway's battlefields and hospitals. In such places, how is one day different from another? Time therefore became an individual and obviously arbitrary matter. Temporal structure changed, place became more important, and the self seemed more anarchistic and precious, less civilized and more instinctual. The self was not identi-fied with the gratifications of work or the luxuries of ocean liners but with the simple, minimal pleasures of a clean, well-lighted place or the sweet and special individuality of the other victims, the "delec-table mountains."

The best book on this generation's autobiography is still Malcolm Cowley's *Exile's Return*, perhaps because Cowley wrote his "criticism" from his own experience just as Fitzgerald, Hemingway, Wolfe, and Dos Passos wrote their "fiction" from theirs. Other critics, with the exception of the biographers who have documented these autobi-ographical novels and short stories, have instead praised the aesthet-ic, mythic, or inventive aspects of their achievements. But their contributions to autobiography are surely as great as their contribu-tions to "fiction." They liberated it from the lock step of chronology and the recitation of the insignificant. Why tell of birth and ancestry or anything else unless it immediately matters? Why wait to write about one's experience until one is celebrated, when one can become celebrated by writing? One might live so long. Why not write and examine while the memories are hot? And why keep the taboos against sex and bad behavior, against gossip and the exposure of one's friends? One need only substitute some fictional names, change dates and places. The novels of the Russian and French realists had already done many of these same things, but the explosion of autobiographical "fictions" by American writers in the 1920s and '30s was more inspiringly personal. It affected the tastes and behavior of its readers like no other books since *Childe Harold* and *The Sorrows of Young Werther*. The writers reported life; the readers imitated art.

Yet, as Malcolm Cowley noted, these writers were spectators. They resisted identification with the civilization in which they lived and so, with few exceptions, did little to try to change it. They preferred to experiment and document and thus alter their world, if at all, through "art." No matter how autobiographical or biographical and documentary their "art," "art" was still above politics and propaganda. And the position of the "artist," even in the 1930s, was still somehow detached. To report, he had to come out as someone detached as well as concerned. So there is detachment and experimentation even in the most explicit autobiography. Gertrude Stein's self-portrait through the eyes of Alice B. Toklas and Conrad Aiken's *Ushant*, where fantasy and history merge in a timeless dream voyage, are two examples. But by these means the avant-garde leaders of this generation certainly did change autobiography just as they changed prose and poetic "fiction," often in the same works.

Full appreciation of more recent American autobiography, by the third generation since Adams, is impossible without recognition of this deep plowing and harrowing and planting. It is, to be sure, the work of a diverse group of writers (as I here lump them together): from Norman Mailer to Alex Haley and Malcolm X, from Jack Kerouac and Allen Ginsberg to Robert Lowell and James Baldwin, and including Sylvia Plath, Mary McCarthy, Scott Momaday, Frank Conroy, Vance Bourjaily, Willie Morris, Lillian Hellman, and many others. But it is the very diversity of their work and the difficulty of assimilating it into one coherent tradition which has frustrated many readers and forced us to look at the history of autobiography, instead of just the history of the novel. Very few of their books—perhaps only *The Autobiography of Malcolm X*—could have been written without the innovations of the preceding generation. As John W. Aldridge testified in *After the Lost Generation*, the writers of this generation grew up in the shadow of giants. But the conclusive evidence of the giants' influence is in Norman Mailer's *Advertisements for Myself* (even though it is now out of print and displaced by *The Armies of the Night* and Mailer's other later works of personal journalism). Mailer could not best Hemingway as a "novelist" for the simple reason that the full title was for the "novelist" as person, as autobiographical hero and clown and performer. The concept of the self as independent critic and adversary of modern civilization could not be articulated in "fiction" alone. It required stances, self-display, and the many other rhetorical devices of the public man. Thus *Advertisments for Myself* is almost a textbook of autobiographical forms—apoligias, personal essays, interviews (including self-interviews), reflections on earlier work, political manifestos, letters, gossip, and so on. It outraged many of Mailer's fellow writers, but it seems eventually to have helped promote and unify their generation. It broke the ice. Many other kinds of self-disclosure have since become more possible.

Another kind of disclosure in this generation (especially in books published in the last ten or fifteen years) is the experience of people whose ancestors were not within the pale of "civilization" as the earlier generations recognized it. The black, ethnic, and feminist autobiographies have broken through the walls of race and sex which so invidiously defined the old "civilization." In doing so, they revived the tradition of autobiography and protest and the use of autobiography to establish the writer's self-concept. Autobiography as history and documentary has an ultimate value no novel or drama, no fiction can ever have. Behind is a person, a living or once-living woman or man. It says, to adapt Whitman's well-known words, "I am the woman, I suffered, I was there." And the person, as opposed to the necessary but dangerous imitations of fiction, will not be a "convention." The "person" uses "convention" as a synonym for "stereotype," for all the non-persons "I" am not. But beyond protest is the joy of being able to say "I am" and who I am. *I Know Why the Caged Bird Sings, A Different Woman, An Unfinished Woman, Manchild in the Promised Land*—the delight and sorrow, the ironies and humor of self are in the very titles of these autobiographies. A person who has found his or her self has, in fact, found something like the *humor* of old medical theory: one's special combination of elements, of blood and history, earth and fire, of which one is made.

So self-advertisement and disclosure are not the only purposes of these autobiographies. Public figures though they be, the authors have not been mere good, honest political candidates obediently revealing all their holdings before assuming public trust. For writers, fortunately, that is not required. It might rob writers, as private persons, of the mysteries which still exist in themselves and which are still lurking in even the most open autobiographies. The paradox of vision is that it cannot be used, cannot change and cure until it is shown; but if it is fully shown, the possessor may lose all personal power. So it may be more appropriate to characterize these autobiographers as having widened the areas of public trust, as having broken the old restrictive civilization, and its dangerous assumption that it alone offered a rewarding life. They have extended concepts of self and of society at the same time. They have made their personal dreams and nightmares a part of the public discourse. Rather than consult the statistics and opinion surveys, they have counseled with their own pasts and personal needs. In an age of threatening depersonalization, when, paradoxically, everyone wants to find his/her "identity," the autobiographer is a hero...or another one of the antiheroes.

The Self as History:
Reflections on Autobiography

by Alfred Kazin

> Every man has reminiscences which he would not tell to everyone, but only to his friends. He has other matters in his mind which he would not reveal even to his friends, but only to himself, and that is secret. But there are other things which a man is afraid to tell even to himself, and every decent man has a number of such things stored away in his mind. The more decent he is, the greater the number of such things in his mind. ... A true autobiography is almost an impossibility... man is bound to lie about himself.
>
> DOSTOEVSKY: NOTES FROM UNDERGROUND

> Whoever undertakes to write a biography binds himself to lying, to concealment, to flummery, and even to hiding his own lack of understanding, since biographical material is not to be had, and if it were it could not be used. Truth is not accessible; mankind does not deserve it, and wasn't Prince Hamlet right when he asked who would escape a whipping if he had his deserts?
>
> SIGMUND FREUD

> We are all special cases.
>
> ALBERT CAMUS

I do not know what "autobiography" is; the genre changes with each new example. What I have tried to write in *A Walker in the City, Starting Out in the Thirties, New York Jew,* is personal history,

"The Self as History: Reflections on Autobiography" by Alfred Kazin. From Marc Pachter, ed., *Telling Lives, The Biographer's Art* (Washington, D.C.: New Republic Books, 1979), pp. 75-89. Reprinted by permission of Alfred Kazin and New Republic Books.

a form of my own influenced by the personal writings of Emerson, Thoreau, Whitman. Its passion and beat come from my life in history, recorded since I was a boy in notebooks that I value not for their facts but for the surprise I attain by writing to myself and for myself. "I write for myself and strangers," said Gertrude Stein. The strangers, dear reader, are an afterthought.

In my experience, Americans sooner or later bring any discussion around to themselves. The American writers with whom, more than any others, I have lived my spirtual life tend to project the world as a picture of themselves even when they are not writing directly about themselves. No doubt this has much to do with the emphasis on the self in America's ancestral Protestantism. Theology in America tends to be Protestant. The self remains the focal point of American literary thinking. From Jonathan Edwards to Hemingway we are confronted by the primitive and unmediated self arriving alone on the American strand, then battling opposing selves who share with us only the experience of being an American.

The deepest side of being an American is the sense of being like nothing before us in history—often enough like no one else around us who is not immediately recognized as one of our tradition, faith, culture, profession. "*What do you do, bud?*" is the poignant beginning of American conversation, "Who are *you*? What am I to expect from *you*?" put into history's language, means that I am alone in a world that was new to begin with and that still feels new to me because the experience of being so *much* a "self"—constantly explaining oneself and telling one's own story—is as traditional in the greatest American writing as it is in a barroom.

What is being talked about is inevitably oneself as a creature of our time and place, the common era that is the subject of history. Every American story revolving around the self, even Henry Miller as a derelict in Paris, is a story of making it against a background symbolically American. Miller made it to Paris after years of being an indistinguishable big-city nobody. In Paris this American nobody wrote himself up as somebody, a symbol of the free life. The point of the story—as it was for Ben Franklin arriving in Philadelphia, Emerson crossing "a bare common" in ecstasies at his newly recognized spiritual powers, Whitman nursing the helpless wounded soldiers in the Civil War hospitals, Henry Adams in awe of the dynamo at the 1900 Paris exposition, E. E. Cummings observing his fellow prisoners in *The Enormous Room*, Hemingway in Parisian cafes writing about his boyhood in Upper Michigan—is that he is making a book out of it, a great book, an exemplary tale of some initiating and original accomplishment that could have been imagined only in an American book. The background seems to say that although the creative spirit is peculiarly alone in America, it is alone *with* America. Here the self, the active, partisan, acquisitive self, born of society, is forever remaking itself, but not in the direction that Keats called "a vale of soul-making."

We tend to emphasize the self as a creature of history and history as a human creation. Even Emerson, the last truly religious, God-oriented writer we have had, the last to believe that the world exists entirely *for* the individual and that "Nature is meant to serve," even Emerson wobbles on the ultimate existence of the individual soul, feels easier with a universal cloud cover called the "Oversoul" than he does with the traditional religious soul in God's keeping, i.e., the soul as the human index and analog of a spiritual world. What Emerson is talking about in *Nature, The American Scholar, The Divinity School Address*, is the "active soul" of the writer as a teacher to humanity. Emerson, whose doctrine gave full faith and comfort to rugged individualism, is a great modern writer not yet altogether secularized. He despises fiction, calls poet and prophet interchangeable terms, *preaches* the necessity to leave the church behind and find God in one's "immeasurable mind." Yet Emerson was so typically double-sighted that he also wrote the first great American book on the old country—*English Traits*. How strange that the same man, in his journals as well as in his famous lectures on everything at large, nevertheless plays the preacher. What he habitually says is that he has taken himself out of the church, out of formal Christianity, in order to prove that one man, by himself, can be a bridge to divine truth.

And that man is you, my fellow American. You can become as great an artist in words as Ralph Waldo Emerson: All you have to do is become a church to yourself and preach from your own immortal genius. July 15, 1838, a Sunday evening before the senior class at Divinity College, Harvard:

> And now, my brothers, you will ask, What in these desponding days can be done by us?...
> Wherever a man comes, there comes revolution. The old is for slaves. When a man comes, all books are legible, all things transparent, all

religions are forms. ... Yourself a newborn bard of the Holy Ghost, cast behind you all conformity and acquaint man at first hand with Deity...Live with the pleasure of the immeasurable mind.

America itself seemed immeasurable in opportunity: "Nature," which meant everything outside of man, existed to serve man on this continent. An American armed with the primacy of the self can do anything. Especially in words. Like Emerson, he can invent a religion just for free spirits and call it literature. Like Thoreau, he can turn a totally lonely life, the death of his beloved brother John, his penny-pinching, lung-destroying, graphite-owning family, into the most beautiful prose fable we have of man perfectly at home with nature. Like Whitman, who took self-revelation as his basic strategy, he can propose a whole new self—which for millions he has become. Whitman, who wrote a great book in the form of a personal epic, compelled and still compels many readers to believe him not only the desperado poet he was but one of the supreme teachers of a troubled humanity. And then in prose, this worldly failure used the Civil War as an abundant backdrop to his picture of himself as tending the wounded soldiers, an American St. Francis who reincarnated himself as a poet, thanks to war and the assassination on Good Friday of his beloved Lincoln. Henry Adams in the *Education*, reverses his loneliness as a widower, his isolation as an historical imagination, into the exquiste historical myth of a Hamlet kept from his rightful kingship—a Hamlet too good for Denmark—a Hamlet who nevertheless knew everybody in the world worth knowing—a Hamlet who finally turned the tables on science, the only knowledge worth having. Adams's last superlative myth is a world that in the twelfth century stood still to worship the Virgin but in the twentieth is racing madly, whirling into outer space in its lust to satisfy Emerson's "immeasurable mind" —intellectual power.

Henry James in his autobiographical prefaces to his collected works and in that staggering personal reverie over what the New World has become, *The American Scene*, showed what mastership over the visible world the literary American self could attain. William James in the personal testimony that is among the most valuable sections of that Emersonian manual in spiritual self-help, *The Varieties of Religious Experience*, showed—in the classic pattern of Protestant autobiography from *Pilgrim's Progress* to John Woolman's *Journal* —that a basic function of such writing is to cure oneself of guilt and self-division.

William James was not the first psychiatrist in America, though he was the student and colleague of those at Harvard who helped to inaugurate this still indefinable therapy. But Dr. James was a genius — it was his best gift — at putting himself together again, in words. "To heal thyself" is a classic reason for a worried man's becoming a physician, especially a psychiatrist. But no psychologist to my knowledge confessed his divided self so eloquently as did William James; no other has so clearly erected a whole system of *belief* to deal with it. James is Emerson's true successor at the end of the century. Emerson never confessed to doubts and was, as Henry James, Sr., said bitterly, a man impossible to get hold of, "without a handle." William James more than anyone in his time understood the American idea that religion helps us shed our sickness, especially in books.

Hemingway was to say that the only psychiatrist *he* needed was a Smith-Corona. But Hemingway, like Saul Bellow in our day, used his own experience obsessively in the form of fiction. So Hemingway kept up the pose to the end that he was invulnerable, famous for "grace under pressure," until the gun in his mouth made it too late for him to admit that his public pose was one great fiction. For the nonfiction writer, as I can testify, personal history is directly an effort to find salvation, to make one's own experience come out right. This is as true of Edmund Wilson in his many autobiographical essays and notebooks as it is of James Baldwin, Malcolm X, Caude Brown. It is even true of straight autobiography by fiction writers. Hemingway's account of his apprenticeship to letters in Paris, *A Moveable Feast*, is an effort to save himself by recovering an idyllic past. Fiction is never simply autobiography — not when it is written by a genuine novelist. The autobiographical impulse in fiction takes the form of satire, burlesque, grandiose mythology, as in *Moby-Dick*. It often mocks the hero and the novel form itself; it generally becomes something altogether different from autobiography by introducing so many other leading characters.

Even the most lasting autobiographies — St. Augustine, Rousseau, Henry Adams — tend to be more case histories limited to the self, as its own history to begin with, than the self as the history of a particular moment and crisis in human history. Saul Bellow has written only one novel, *The Victim*, in which he has not sat for a leading character. Sammler and Charles Citrine, Herzog, and even Henderson represent Bellow in various stages of his life, different moods, different wives. But there are so many other people and points of interest in his novels, like the frolicsome portrait of the poet Delmore Schwartz in *Humboldt's Gift*, that it is clear that what makes the human comedy balance out right is the creative process for this self-renewing novelist, not Bellow's own history.

Still, wholly personal documents like Whitman's *Specimen Days*, Adams's *Education*, Conrad Aiken's *Ushant*, Malcolm X's *Autobiography*, can be more lasting than many a novel. What preserves such books is the news they bring us of history in a new form. In every notable case of this form, from Franklin's *Autobiography* to Richard Wright's *Black Boy* and Frederick Exley's *A Fan's Notes*, we have the epic of personal struggle, a situation rather than a plot. The writer turns himself into a representative sinner or Christian or black or Jew —in Exley's case a comically incurable drunk.

This person, we say to ourselves as we encounter Franklin arriving in Philadelphia, has *lived* history. These are people recounting their fame. Here is Edward Gibbon: "It was at Rome, on the 15th of October 1764, as I sat musing amid the ruins of the Capitol, while the barefooted friars were singing vespers in the temple of Jupiter, that the idea of writing the decline and fall of the city first started to my mind." But Gibbon's book is all about how important he was; he is incapable of making fun of himself. It is not from his innocently pompous memoirs that we learn that the great historian, as a member of Parliament from a rotten borough, fell asleep during the debates on the American Revolution. One can *live* history in a quite different way, as witness Franklin's comic account of himself walking up Market Street, carrying two rolls, eating a third, and seeing his future wife "when she standing at the Door saw me, and thought I made as I certainly did a most awkward ridiculous Appearance."

To "live" history is not of course to command it, or even one's fate in life. To live history is to express most memorably a relationship to the past, to a particular setting, to a moment, sometimes even to a particular set of buildings, as Henry James does so vibrantly in that travel book of sheer genius, *The American Scene*, where buildings are talking to one another because James's mind is so busily interogating them.

My favorite example of history-to-the-life is Henry Adams's account of being taken as a boy to Washington. He has already told us in many indirect and delightful ways that he is the grandson and great-grandson of presidents. He is staying with his grandmother, widow of John Quincy Adams:

Coming down in the early morning from his bedroom in his grand-mother's house—still called the Adams building—in F Street and venturing outside into air reeking with the thick odor of the catalpa trees, he found himself on the earth-road, or village street, with wheel tracks meandering from the colonnade of the Treasury hard by, to the white marble columns and fronts of the Post Office and Patent Office which faced each other in the distance, like white Greek temples in the abandoned gravel-pits of a deserted Syrian city.

This is a passage of historical music. The key words are sacred names, as Proust said of Combray, as Gibbon rang the litany of historical names in the great passage enumerating Rome, the ruins of the Capitol, barefooted friars singing vespers in the temple of Jupiter. Adams is also rendering the art of history by locating himself as a boy of twelve wandering from the house of "Madame President" through the ancient sleepy undistinguished unfinished Washington of 1850. Unlike Gibbon's Rome, all in ruins, Adams's Washington is seen by *us* as the powerful America of the future, but strangely ignorant of its future as we see the earth-road, the village streets, wheeltracks. But note that the Treasury has a Greek colonnade and, a most rewarding detail, the white marble columns and fronts of the Post Office and Patent Office in the distance face each other like white Greek temples in the abandoned gravel-pits of a deserted Syrian city. The innocently pompous all-marble Washington of the future, where Adams wrote this passage in 1905 sitting in his great house just across Lafeyette Square from the White House, must contend in our minds with the beautifully supple historical imagination of Adams the great historian picturing Syria forgotten in the ruins of the Roman Empire.

When Adams wrote this passage America had just acquired, out of the goodness of its heart, the Philippines, Puerto Rico, Cuba. Adams's sometime friend Theodore Roosevelt, whom he amusedly tolerated as a gentleman from his own set (he thought the president insane), was enjoying the presidency with unholy zest. The moment had al-ready come at the great Paris exposition of 1900 when Adams dis-covered that his "historical back" was broken by the sight of the dynamo:

The planet itself seemed less impressive, its old-fashioned, deliberate, annual or daily revolution, than this huge wheel, revolving within arm's length at some vertiginous speed, and barely murmuring— scarcely humming an audible warning to stand a hair's breadth further for respect of power—while it would not wake the baby lying close against its frame. Before the end, one began to pray to it; inherited instinct taught the natural expression of man before silent and infinite force. ...

This is the self living history as its own fate. The barely murmuring dynamo will turn soon into the rocket, Adams into Norman Mailer at Cape Kennedy awed by the towering hangar built to house the moon rocket. The mountebank in the White House, Theodore Roosevelt, will become the succession of presidents after Vietnam unable to halt their own powerlessness. History as our own fate is what the grandiose theoretical last chapters of the *Education* have to teach us. And that is the deepest meaning of "autobiography," historically considered. Adams in Washington, 1850, yields to Adams in Washington, 1900, to ourselves in Washington and New York in 2000. The infinite universe mocks the American belief that its power is constant and growing, surrounded by empires without our ancient belief in the goodness of all people brought up under constitutional democracy.

Walt Whitman is another great example of the self living history— first as a mere spectator; then as our common fate, history as the ultimate explanation of our individual fortunes in life. In *Song of Myself* Whitman wrote of the hstorical visions he painted of America at mid-century—"*I am the man, I suffer'd, I was there.*" In his great diary of the Civil War, *Specimen Days*, Whitman describes himself going down to Washington to look for his brother George, wounded in the second battle of Bull Run. What Whitman does not say is that he was at his lowest ebb as poet and man. *Leaves of Grass* had failed, he really had nothing to occupy himself with at the moment, and he must have had an instinct that the war would be one of those historical tragedies in which the rejected of history find their souls again, in which the epics of the race are reborn.

Early in *Specimen Days* Walt Whitman describes the beaten Federal soldiers in retreat lying along the streets of Washington. Only Whitman would have caught the peculiar poignance of the contrast between the marble Capitol and the helpless, often neglected suffering in what was now a very confused capital. The most splendid instance of Whitman's eye picking out such historical ironies is the description of the wounded soldiers lying in the Patent Office:

A few weeks ago the vast area of the second story of that noblest of Washington buildings was crowded close with rows of sick, badly wounded and dying soldiers. They were placed in three very large apartments. I went there many times. It was strange, solemn, and with all its features of suffering and death, a sort of fascinating sight. .... Two of the immense apartments are filled with high and ponderous glass cases, crowded with models in miniature of every kind of utensil,machine, or invention it ever entered into the mind of man to conceive; and with curiosities and foreign presents. .... It was indeed a curious scene, especially at night when lit up. The glass cases, the beds, the forms lying there, the gallery above, and the marble pavement underfoot...

Whitman does not neglect to tell us at the end of this description of the Patent Office that the wounded soldiers have now been all removed. There *was* an historical moment; he was there. Just in time to record fully the typical American contrast between our technical genius and what war does. Whitman was not a soldier, not even a real nurse. History may well wonder if he gave as much to the soldiers as they gave him. They made possible his great poems and prose of the war. But there is present in *Specimen Days* and in the cycle of war poems, *Drum-Taps*, a kind of historical light or atmosphere that is extraordinary. It is a quality one finds only in the greatest books— from the *Iliad* to *War and Peace*— that show history itself as a character. A certain light plays on all the characters, the light of what we call history. And what is history in this ancient sense but the commemoration of our common experience, the unconscious solidarity of a people celebrated in the moments of greatest stress, as the Bible celebrates over and again history as the common experience of the race, from creation to redemption?

But something new has entered into twentieth-century experience. We no longer identify ourselves *with* history. Joyce's Stephen Dedalus said, "History is the nightmare from which I am trying to awaken." History since 1914 has become for the "educated classes" of the West not so much a memory as a threat. This may be one reason for the marked failure of "history" to awaken enthusiasm or even much intellectual curiosity among the young. To have a sense of history one must consider *oneself* a piece of history. Although our age will be remembered most of all for the endless multiplication of technological innovation and scientific information, the "feel" of the present—

at least to the white middle class that still writes its history as the history of the world—is that history is out of control, beyond all the prophecies and calculations made for it in the nineteenth century, when the organization of industrial society was plainly the pattern of the future. Hence the unconscious despair of people whose first legend is the city of peace built on a hill, a new world to be born, a new man to be made.

But to the others, who are just arising in history and for whom history is their effort alone, the self knows history only as nemesis and liberation from oppression. Hence, in our immediate culture we get more and more a view of literature as political rhetoric. Imaginative literature even in our privileged society is now so much under the pressure of journalism, documentary, the media, the daily outrage and atrocity, and above all unconscious mass fright, that autobiography of one kind or another, often the meanest travel report through contemporary life, has become all too fashionable and omni-present.

On every hand I seem to see people saying *I am the man, I got the story first, I was there.* Even that miserable schemer who tape-recorded himself out of the presidency had no higher aim than to write a best-seller called *Nixon as History*. The public gets more and more submissive to instant history. Looking at the endless news reports on television, we resemble savages cowering from the storm in their caves, waiting on the gods to decide our fate. Society, as we draw to the end of our century, resembles the primitive idea of nature as reward or punishment. The man on the spot may only be a ventriloquist's dummy, like most news commentators, reading what he has been given to read. But literature essentially does nothing different when it appeals, as our most gifted writers do, only to the public experience of politics, the moon voyage, the political assassination, the seeming irreconcilability of the sexes.

The real problem for "personal history" now is how to render this excess of outer experience as personal but not private experience. This is the feminine tradition, and women writers know better than men how to turn the glib age of incessant reportage back into personal literature. But there is at the same time so clamorous a cry of personal weakness, so much confessional poetry and fiction, that I ask myself, as a "personal historian," what the spell is on all of us—not least our readers. For of course Plath, Lowell, Berryman, Rich, Olsen, Duncan, Ginsberg, Sexton, Wakoski would not have written such texts, would not be the stars of the classroom nowadays if there were not so many readers who seem to read no poetry and prose that is not confessional, who demand that literature be about the confessional self—an invitation to become confessional themselves.

Does this mean that the theme I began with, the autobiographer as a triumph over his own life, has changed into the self-proclaimed disaster? Of course not. Confession is possible, even popular. We live in a society whose standards of personal conduct have been mocked by all our recent presidents, to say nothing of our leading corporation executives. The open lust for political advantage over human rights and belief in our American superpowers have made breakdown and confession, Vietnam, Watergate and investigation a pattern of our time.

Erik Erikson says that all confession is an effort to throw off a curse. Guilt seems more endemic than it ever did. It is certainly more popular. Why? No doubt it makes possible a confessional literature that is self-dramatizing in the absence of moral authority. At the same time the dramatization of the self in American literature goes back to a very old theme. How well have *I* made out? What am I to think of *my* life, all things considered? Could it have been any different? Let us not deceive ourselves: Each person, especially in this historically still most hopeful of countries, is constantly making up the progress report of his life, and knows that in this respect everyone we know, love, and hate, everyone to whom we have ever been tied, shares our interests exactly—this life, my life, this time...

So the anxious but somehow thrivingly preoccupied self, in a culture where personal fortune and happiness are more real than God has become even to many believers, cannot help connecting himself with people like himself in this period, with a history that betrays the most intimate passions. Once gods of the earth, presidents now seem all too much like ourselves. More and more the sexes are compelled to admit that men and women—alas!—are more alike than we had dreamed, egotists before anything else. Everywhere we turn we seem to be within the same bedroom walls, under pressure from the same authorities. Hence, not equality but *identity* becomes the condition of life as we get mashed into shape by the same corporations, shopping plazas, ranch houses, mass universities, television programs, instant replay of the same public atrocities.

In all this the self becomes freely articulate about itself, recognizing a *psychological* bond with other selves that is negative. Every confession becomes a progress report of the most intense interest to others. And if the confession is an attempt to ward off a curse, writing it out is also a boast: to be able to write one's life, to make one's way successfully through so many ghosts, between so many tombs, is indeed a boast.

All I have to boast about is that I have at least tried to express my life. I have been saved by language. My sixty years have been lived directly *and* symbolically in the storm centers of the twentieth century. Nothing seems more remote than the illusion of security and tranquillity as the century accelerates the violence and nihilism that have marked all our lives since 1914-1918 showed that the concentrated power of modern weapons can be even more suicidal than private despair.

Yet I believe that history exists, that it is still meaningful, and that we can read our fate in the book of history. That gives me the courage to write. To write is in some way to cut the seemingly automatic pattern of violence, destructiveness, and death wish. To write is to put the seeming insignificance of human existence into a different perspective. It is the need, the wish, and, please God, the ability to reorder our physical fate by mental means, a leap of the imagination, an act of faith. Wallace Stevens once wondered in an essay whether it is not "the violence within that protects us from the violence without." The "violence within" is the effort to make a mental construct that shall hang together—that shall be within the inner landscape a seamless and uninterruptable web—that can prove, as Henry James said, that "the whole truth about anything is never told; we can only take what groups together."

Violence is distinguished by gaps, discontinuties, inconsistency, confusion condensed into power—but no less blind and chaotic for that. The life of mere experience, and especially of history as the supposedly total experience we ridiculously claim to know, can seem an inexplicable series of unrelated moments. But language, even when it is most a mimicry of disorder, is distinguished from violence, atrocity, deceit, by relating word to word, sentence to sentence, thought to thought—man to this final construct on a page— always something different from mere living.

So that is why I write, to reorder an existence that man in the mass will never reorder for me. Even autobiography is a necessary stratagem to gain something more important than itself. By the time experience is distilled enough through our minds to set some particular thing down on paper, so much unconscious reordering has gone on that even the naive wish to be wholly "truthful" fades before the intoxication of line, pattern, form.

Stephen Crane said that art is a child of pain. Existence is itself an anxious matter for many Americans in the twentieth century precisely because the material power is greatest in this country; we have had the greatest illusion of control. And so the disappointment and anger are greater still. In the writing of our time and place, one sees a greater questioning, philosophical and moral rootlessness, a despair that is often just the other side of the most romantic and reckless hope. So the self becomes the accuser, as it so often seems only the target—the self adrift in a private universe. This, to Americans caught off base, as we all are now, can seem as frightening as the silence of those infinite spaces seemed to Pascal:

> When I consider the short duration of my life, swallowed up in the eternity before and after, the little space which I fill, and even can see, engulfed in the infinite immensity of spaces of which I am ignorant, and which know me not, I am frightened, and am astonished at being here rather than there; for there is no reason why *here* rather than *there*, why *now* rather than *then*. Who has put me here? By whose order and direction have this place and time been allotted to me?

So one writes to make a home for oneself, on paper, despite Milton's *blind Fury with the abhorréd shears, who slits the thin-spun life.* In our time history, too, can be "the blind Fury." But to write is to live it again, and in this personal myth and resurrection of our experience, to give honor to our lives.

Stages of Self:
Notes on Autobiography and the Life Cycle

by Patricia Meyer Spacks

Why do autobiographies now sound so different from those of the nineteenth and eighteenth centuries? We think vaguely that *people* sounded different in the past, and we are doubtless right. Yet autobiographies raise some special questions. One might explore, for example, their systematic exclusions: the sorts of material that writers in different periods choose to omit from accounts of themselves; or one could start by looking into the modes of self-justification acceptable for memoirists in various eras. Benjamin Franklin tells us that he writes only for the moral edification of his descendants; Virgil Thomson, in our own day, feels more comfortable informing his lecture audiences that he wrote his autobiography simply for the sake of money. A matter of fashion, such poses; but fashions, of course, bear meanings.

And fashions in autobiography affect every conceivable aspect of the genre—if, indeed, it *is* a genre: some critics prefer to think of it as an attitude, a state of mind. One might examine with profit the shifting ways in which autobiographers deal with the subsidiary characters in their life stories: how important do other people seem and why? Or one could look into the various rhetorics available to self-describers and the kinds of effect facilitated by different styles of language; or compare recorded self-images from various ethnic groups, economic circumstances, nationalities. Historical generalizations can be made, I feel confident, about all such matters. Like all generalizations—like, for instance, the ones I am about to elaborate—they would not be flawless: autobiographers do not unani

"Stages of Self: Notes on Autobiography and the Life Cycle" by Patricia Meyer Spacks. From *Boston University Journal*, 25, no. 2 (1977), 7-17. Reprinted by permission of the author.

mously change tactics as a new century starts. Moreover, all writers have more or less available to them the resources of the past, slipping into old languages or modes of perception often with an astonishing air of comfort. We keep rediscovering our predecessors in our contemporaries. I would be surprised if anyone could show me an eighteenth-century autobiography so far in advance of its time as to dwell in loving detail on the experiences of childhood, but not at all surprised to be reminded of works from our own day which fall into the rhetoric or employ the masks more typical of previous centuries. The generalization that the realistic novel is dead cannot be refuted by pointing to a recent realistic novel: in literature if not in life, nothing completely dies; on the other hand, individual survivals may only emphasize the essential demise of a species.

Nothing I am able to say, then, will characterize all autobiographies of a given period; I wish instead to offer a rather impressionistic view of a general pattern of historical change. The development I see correlates precisely with a famous observation by the historian of childhood, Philippe Ariès. "It is as if," he says, "to every period of history there corresponded a privileged age and a particular division of human life." For the nineteenth century, the special age is childhood; for the twentieth, adolescence. Ariès fails to characterize the eighteenth century, but one can readily observe how insistently that era glorified full maturity—meaning by that the capacity to behave like a person governed by reason, fulfilling effectively some more or less public role. Men writing about their lives in the new Augustan age—my use of the masculine designation is deliberate, for reasons which will soon become apparent—slide over the events of their childhoods to stress the achievements of adulthood. Only a limited range of feelings could be relevant to such accounts. A hundred years later, John Ruskin would devote almost half a thousand-page autobiography to the happenings and emotions of his early years, referring to himself as a child until he is far along in what we would call adolescence. And stormy adolescence itself creates the conventional center of interest for a great many twentieth-century reminiscences. What happens in adolescence *matters,* we believe; our forefathers believed this far less fervently.

Looking into the eighteenth century's fascination with maturity, we must recall how the period's views of psychology were dominated by John Locke, who had postulated that the human mind at birth constitutes a blank tablet, gradually to be filled by the accumulated sense impressions and associations of experience. What happens to the child therefore has considerable importance (theories of education accordingly burgeoned at the time), yet the incompletely formed juvenile mind can hardly claim the same kind of attention or respect as the fully formed adult intellect, and no one had yet imagined grounds for valuing the child's state even more highly than the adult's. The theory of psychological development conveyed by eighteenth-century writers on education implies that "natural" human development leads from childhood innocence to adolescent self-indulgence, the principle of growth within each individual dangerously intensifying the power of the passions, which grows more rapidly than that of reason. The passions, in Alexander Pope's formulation, are "Modes of Self-love," fundamental impulses to action which, unchecked, would cause man "meteor-like, [to] flame lawless thro' the void, Destroying others, by himself destroy'd." Moral education, guided by adult rationality, must center on moderating, restraining, controlling the passions, thus interfering rather than cooperating with the natural course of development. "Attention, habit and experience," to quote Pope once more, strengthen reason, thus moving man toward maturity. And everyone wishes to become adult as soon as possible—such was the general assumption—although everyone also dreads old age. A *Spectator* essay by Richard Steele begins by announcing these ideas as universal truths: "Age is so unwelcome to the generality of mankind, and growth toward manhood so desirable to all..."

Growth toward manhood seemed so desirable, in fact, that many autobiographers in effect denied their childhoods, eliding their early years into a few anecdotes susceptible of moral interpretation. The pattern is familiar enough from eighteenth-century fiction: *Tom Jones,* for example, purports to relate its hero's career from birth, yet the leisurely narrative pauses only briefly over the childhood years. Smollett, Richardson, Fanny Burney: all interest themselves in the experience of young men or women, but not in that of children. Even Tristram Shandy in all his verbosity offers only isolated exemplary anecdotes of the years between infancy and young manhood. Just so with autobiographies. William Cowper, in the memoir recounting his religious salvation, reports, along with two episodes of early religious stirrings, only some fragmentary evidence of his youthful misery and isolation before he puts his trust in God. His very different contemporary, John Harriott—sailor, adventurer, inventor—tells only two stories of his childhood; both involve stealing and subsequent pangs of conscience. The life story of the well-known clergyman Thomas Somerville effectively begins at the age of eleven, with a detailed account of what he was taught at school and how; he claims for himself at that age no individuality whatever. Such eighteenth-century autobiographers assert only a vague childhood reality apparently derived from moralistic fiction or from other literary sources; seldom does it possess the emotional vibrancy which we associate with long-preserved memory. Childhood matters, in these narratives, inasmuch as it foretells maturity; it has no claimed intrinsic value in memory or in narration.

Adulthood, on the other hand, can be assumed to attract the reader's interest—not for what the protagonist has felt, or for what he is, but for what he has done. Benjamin Franklin, probably the best-known American autobiographer of his century, is typical in his assumptions if not in all his techniques. Readers will interest themselves in his story, he believes, because they know of his accomplishments in the world, which give him authority, assure his right to demand attention. Across the Atlantic, the historian Edward Gibbon (who never completed his autobiography to his own satisfaction) declared his intention of explaining how he achieved professional success, selecting material from his life for its relevance to the making of a historian's mind. The agriculturalist Arthur Young oddly combines an account of religious conversion with detailed records of plans, accomplishments, rewards, and unmerited failures as farmer and writer about farming. The actor Colley Cibber, the philosopher David Hume, the bookseller James Lackington—all reveal the same faith that the psychological and moral development of the civilized man is attested by books written or sold, stage performances produced or acted, things done in public. Ardent religious faith, of course, might shift a man's orientation toward his private relation with God—it does so in Cowper, one feels it tugging at Young. But the normal course of progress took one from the relative ostracism of childhood, forbidden to dine with the grown-ups, to triumphant socialization. The century's autobiographers, like its moralists, saw themselves primarily as social beings, using accounts of their personal experience to declare not only uniqueness—although Hume, Cibber, Gibbon, Lackington all proclaim their specialness—but the degree to which they partake in and contribute to a society of adults, function as *citizens*.

I have dealt only with men thus far; and Steele declared the desirability of growth toward manhood, not womanhood. Women in the eighteenth century were socialized even earlier, and far more rigorously, than men. Their natural development too was assumed to lead them from insentience to passion, but the danger of passion was felt to be far greater for women, the need for repression consequently more intense. The relatively few autobiographical records by women written during the century accordingly convey a rather different attitude from men's about the stages of life. For men, adult life, despite its social responsibilities, provided the arena of freedom and expressiveness. For women, adulthood—marriage or spinster-hood—implied relative loss of self. Unlike men, therefore, they looked back fondly to the relative freedom and power of childhood and youth. Charlotte Charke, Colley Cibber's daughter, herself an experimenter at profit-making activities ranging from stage acting to selling fish, reminisces about her childish wiles and exploits and their effect on her father. That father, in his own autobiography, remembers only childhood episodes foretelling his future; Mrs. Charke recalls that everything seemed possible in the early days, that her impulses toward independence then won more approval than scorn: later realities revealed her social impotence. Laetitia Pilkington, whose married life proved a nightmare, remembers how her father encouraged her in girlhood, how men flocked around in her adolescence. Her power to attract men proved a liability, given a jealous husband; her literary powers too, source of early praise, caused contention with that husband. Hester Thrale, a writer of voluminous journals rather than of formal autobiography, used a genre traditionally focused on the present moment also as a reposi-tory of reminiscence. She too remembers with nostalgic pleasure the time of life when a girl can use all her capacities to charm men without social disapproval. At ten years old she was thought a prodigy, praised for her intellect and grace; at twenty-five, she was told to mind her babies and not to presume to discuss what she could not understand. Women autobiographers of the eighteenth century often use memoirs to reconstruct the course of life with the emphasis of desire rather than of fact. Although they, like men, proudly report whatever public accomplishments they have to offer, they lay far greater stress on childhood, that period of no accomplishment but of emotional satisfaction.

Nineteenth-century autobiographies are generally longer than their eighteenth-century counterparts—the two-volume, thousand-page work is not uncommon. At first glance the self-renditions of John Ruskin and Herbert Spencer seem like vastly expanded versions of Hume's account of himself, or Gibbon's. They, too, assume their audience's interest in achievement (Spencer, in fact, provides appendices describing his various inventions and theories: an invalid chair, a universal language). But the influence of Jean-Jacques Rousseau had spread since Gibbon's day. At the end of the eighteenth century, Mary Wollstonecraft inveighed against Rousseau; educational theorists attempted to refute him; a hundred years later, his ideas permeated the atmosphere as completely as Freud's views do now. One can argue against Freud, condemn him, modify his theories, but his popularized influence persists far below the level of rational discourse: exactly so with Rousseau, who told the world of the natural goodness of children, the destructive effects of civilization. Childhood, he proclaimed, was, or should be, the happiest time of life. The doctrine encouraged adult nostalgia for vanished bliss as well as having widely diffused effects ranging from permissive experiments in education to Victorian erotic photographs of little girls. (I am, of course, ignoring other causes for these phenomena.)

Ruskin and Spencer, born a year apart, express opposite sides of the nineteenth-century myth of childhood. Ruskin, who refers explicitly to "the perfectly happy time of childhood," also declares his early years "the most seriously eventful for me in good and evil" and assesses himself, at seven years old, as a being of irrevocably determined character. His life up to that time has been virtually perfect; recalling with a kind of ecstasy his infantile interest in a water pipe outside the house or his playing with a bunch of keys, he reports as minor complaints that he was supplied with no outlet for his capacity to love, that he was given no hardship to endure, and that he received little instruction in social graces and little opportunity to develop power of independent action. Speaking of himself at the age of fourteen, he mentions "not wanting to be anything but the boy I was" (what a change from Steele's assumption that all boys yearn to be men!), and asserts, "It is not possible to imagine, in any time of the world, a more blessed entrance into life, for a child of such a temperament as mine." His sense of childhood as a crucial and peculiarly satisfying time of life permeates his book—in which evidence of emotional satisfaction in adult experience is conspicuously absent.

Spencer's autobiography, in contrast, throbs with its author's grievance at having been *deprived* of a happy childhood. His mother always criticized him and "perpetually sacrificed herself unduly"; his father seemed irritable and depressed, checking in himself "that geniality of behavior which fosters the affections." As a consequence, Herbert Spencer disliked his father, although he scrupulously reports a letter from his mother claiming that "in early childhood I had a great fondness for my father." His "most vivid childish recollection," he says, is of the terror and agony of being deserted by his parents and nurse. At the age of thirteen he ran away from his uncle's home, to which he had been consigned, enduring physical hardship which he believes damaged him for life, although there is no evidence for this contention. His anger and resentment at parents, nurse, uncle and aunt, emerge repeatedly. Yet, three hundred pages into the second volume, he declares, "The maxim on which I have acted, and the maxim which I have often commended to my friends is—Be a boy as long as you can." He means, specifically, "Don't give up sports and games," but the formulation surely suggests more. As vividly as Ruskin's obsessive dwelling on his youth, Spencer's complaints declare his belief in the special importance of childhood. Only if a person feels his right to happiness in a given situation can he experience such intense injustice at failing to be given it.

Ruskin and Spencer share precisely that quality conspicuously absent in eighteenth-century autobiographies: a conveyed sense of the self's particular uniqueness in childhood. Ruskin feels his entire family to be remarkable, and he as part of it. Spencer's feeling of personal specialness has a more startling effect, since it directly contradicts his conscious purpose of always trying to derive general laws from specific observations: no generalization will fully account for *him*. His childhood resentment against adult control expresses itself as anger against his parents for their natures and insufficiencies, their manifest incapacity to fill the needs of a being so extraordinary as he, their child. As he moves toward recording his adulthood, the feeling of specialness appears to diminish; the writing accordingly becomes increasingly mechanical and routine.

Not before the nineteenth century do autobiographical accounts have titles like *My Girlhood Days* or *A Nineteenth-Century Childhood*. Both these books, as it happens, are by women, but the difference between the governing ideas of male and female life stories is far less dramatic in the nineteenth century than in the preceding one. I suspect that the mode of grievance is more characteristically masculine (think, for example, of John Stuart Mill), that of celebration more typical of women; but I know of no individual text by a woman so extensively and forcefully affirmative about childhood as Ruskin's narrative. Hearty affirmation, however, abounds. Even the life story of the Victorian feminist Frances Power Cobbe, in which one might expect to find emphasis on adult struggles and accomplishments or on the social oppression of a girl's lot, contains its panegyric on her childhood: "I can recall...feeling as if everything in the world was perfect, and my life complete bliss for which I could never thank God enough."

Men and women alike, a century ago, perceived their experience in relation to an ideal form of human development in which the best comes first. Wordsworth's great autobiographical poem, with its stress on the child's natural communion with all that is most authentic and powerful, strikes a far more characteristic nineteenth-century note than Browning's "Rabbi Ben Ezra," in which the persona invites his listener to "Grow old along with me, The best is yet to be, The last of life for which the first is made." Indeed, the effectiveness of Browning's poetic assertion derives almost entirely from its very improbability: such a statement would be felt as paradox in an era so fully committed to glorification of extreme youth. Rich in innocence and bliss (both terms with significant theological implications), the child had special power; no wonder that adults writing about themselves often strove to recapture it. Thus DeQuincey, writing in 1853 a general preface to his *Autobiographic Sketches,* modestly disclaims importance beyond "amusement" for most of his records of self. At times, however, he grants, "the narrative rises into a far higher key. Most of all it does so at a period of the writer's life where, of necessity, a severe abstraction takes place from all that could invest him with any alien interest; no display that might dazzle the reader, nor ambition that could carry his eye forward with curiosity to the future, nor successes, fixing his eye on the present; nothing on the stage but a solitary infant, and its solitary combat with grief—a mighty darkness, and a sorrow without a voice." This image of the solitary infant focuses for the autobiographer his sense of personal significance; the best that he can hope for his account of his later life is that "perhaps" it may rekindle "something of the same interest." Essentially, though, for the nineteenth-century autobiographer as for the liver of a nineteenth-century life, all progress is understood to be downhill.

Freud disabused us of naive faith in the innocence of children, but not of myths about the shape of life. Erik Erikson—himself, of course, profoundly influential in forming twentieth-century views of human development—has said that one writes autobiography late in life, in order to confirm and solidify a myth of self. But such myths remain (as myths always do) social as well as personal; and the twentieth-century myth of selfhood centers on adolescence—partly, paradoxically, because the adolescent is seen as relatively free from the pressures of society. As Claude Lévi-Strauss observed in *Tristes Tropiques*, "Our adolescents, like those of the North American Indians, are encouraged to get clear, by one means or another, of civilization." Moreover, we encourage ourselves in retrospect to believe that once upon a time we ourselves did get clear. People write their autobiographies now at increasingly early ages; more and more people seem to write them; and more and more often, they concentrate on adolescence. Autobiographies sometimes end with the end of adolescence—some brilliant examples are Maya Angelou's *I Know Why the Caged Bird Sings* (the subsequent autobiographical volume, about her adulthood, has far less force), Frank Conroy's *Stop-Time*, and Mary McCarthy's *Memories of a Catholic Girlhood*—as though everything important had already happened by then. Or they go on and on, like Bertrand Russell's, but lose passion and energy after reporting the adolescent years. Rather than multiply examples, though, of the twentieth-century's autobiographical emphasis on literal adolescence, I'd like to offer some suggestions about the *metaphorical* importance of adolescence in our visions of self.

In some important American autobiographies by men born before the middle of the nineteenth century but living into the twentieth—I'm thinking particularly of Henry Adams and William Dean Howells—one can see vividly the early development of this metaphor of adolescence. Such accounts, emphasizing the pain more than the pleasure of youth, describe the transitional years between childhood and adulthood as a period of crucial importance in determining the narrator's fate—"a space of blind struggle," in Howell's words, "relieved by moments of rest and shot with gleams of light, when the youth, if he is fortunate, gathers some inspiration for a worthier future." The anguish of this time, he explains, comes from the tension between a longing for home and original family and the need to "cleave to the world and the things of it," this being the necessary "condition of all achievement and advancement." In his life as he reports it, the struggle to resolve that tension extends itself well into the years of nominal adulthood. Henry Adams, describing his entire career as a process of education, delineates a prolonged—a virtually endless—adolescent identity crisis. His inability to resolve the question of who he is or can be incapacitates him, or so he claims, until his old age; his resentment directs itself at his family, his country, his historical era, in classic adolescent fashion.

Later writers have sounded more cheerful about adolescence, the proclamation of its hardships providing an apparent part of their literary pleasure. For many adults, adolescence supplies the focus of a particularly compelling set of fantasies. If childhood could be associated, in the last century, with irresponsible and innocent happiness, the ideal state of being cared for and indulged, in our time adolescence means permitted defiance and difference. It means other things too, of course, but its potency as a central image for human development depends heavily on its definition as the period in which one discovers or creates an identity separate from and significantly opposed to that of one's elders: for many, particularly in retrospect, an exciting activity. Adolescence, Erikson has explained, finding words for a general feeling which certainly predated his pronouncement, as writers like Howells testify, is a time of moratorium, a space *between*. Its peculiar freedom allows the young person to oppose the status quo often with relatively little penalty. As we can all remember if we try, it doesn't necessarily feel good to be an adolescent—one feels, in fact, often powerless, baffled, and miserable. But looking from the vantage point of adulthood back at the rising generation, we see figures of gathering power— sexual, physical, ideological—and confidence, young men and women who, unlike ourselves, have not yet given hostages to fortune, do not need to conform. It is possible to see one's own youthful self, too, in such terms, and to admire that particular self above all others.

Why we should tend to admire that version of self is an interesting and complicated question—it is not the image of personality valued a century or two centuries ago. But twentieth-century self-presentations often focus on a personality insistently fluid, insistently at odds with what we now call "the establishment." Consider again, for example, the composer Virgil Thomson as autobiographer. His actual adolescence, he reports, included an episode in which he defied his parents in order to declare his vocation as musician, ignoring the fact that his parents offered no opposition at all; and it included his enlistment in the Army, not out of patriotism but from a "yearning toward novel experience." These two events, archetypal experiences of adolescence, suggest dominant patterns for the rest of his narrative, in which he is ever seeking new experience, ever locating objects of defiance. In his late thirties he received a medal from the Chicago branch of the American Opera Society. He felt, he writes, "a bit ashamed, as if I were being blest by some Establishment." I am not suggesting that he was a thirty-eight-year-old adolescent: only that, like other autobiographers of our time, he uses as an organizing myth an idea of himself strongly associated with the special values of adolescence. One might say precisely the same thing about the vigorous autobiographical writing of Lillian Hellman, who describes herself, with considerable pride, as a life-long rebel; tells with manifest pleasure the story, rich in symbolic power, of literally spitting in Dashiel Hammett's eye; and apparently feels shame mainly about her occasional moments of conformity, of acting the lady. Other examples come readily to mind: Norman Podhoretz, Alfred Kazin, V. S. Pritchett. In one way or another—and the ways, it must be said, are various—many autobiographies of the twentieth century declare the imaginative dominance of the idea of adolescence. Frank Conroy reports of his manhood only gratuitous risk-taking with his car, gambling with his life: as if to say that death represents the only alternative to the atmosphere of challenge and excitement associated with puberty.

Autobiography seems by definition the most personal form of literary expression, rich in potential idiosyncrasy. In our own time, when writers often feel free to reveal their sexual exploits and inhibitions, their intimate animosities, their furtive longings, the genre particularly insists on the uniqueness of the individual's experience and inner life. Yet a recorded revelation of how-I-had-a-love-affair -with-General-Eisenhower fulfills conventional expectations as precisely as did the many accounts, three hundred years ago, of how-I-gave-up-my-unregenerate-life-and-found-salvation-through-Christ; only the conventions differ. Of course, I've been considering more than literary convention in thinking about autobiography in relation to the life cycle. The patterns of emphasis in narratives of the self from different periods reflect commonly held assumptions, like the patterns which shape spiritual autobiography or, in our time, sexual revelation; but the exact source and nature of those assumptions repays further examination.

We have become accustomed by now to the idea that autobiography, no matter how "honest," involves necessary fictions, artifices of self-exposure, masks through which alone the self can be known. Autobiographers realized this fact before critics did; thus Goethe, in conversation with Eckermann (30 March 1831), remarked, speaking of his own autobiography, "A fact of our life has validity not by its being true, but rather by its being significant." The ambiguities about factuality created by such an attitude may generate problems for a reader obsessed with distinguishing literal from imaginative truth; but most sophisticated readers now are accustomed to considering autobiography as part of a continuum also including fiction, the line between fiction and fact difficult and usually unnecessary to draw. We understand the fictions of autobiography as modes of communication, devices for conveying essential truth, part of the ordering process of art.

The notion of the life cycle, in its developed forms, also involves necessary fiction. Our experience of life, obviously, does not proceed by an orderly sequence of clearly distinguished stages. On a particular day we may suddenly realize that we are, or are considered by others, old, or middle-aged, or even adolescent, but no sounding trumpets mark the transition from one category to the next. Even the child who celebrates the arrival of each new pubic hair cannot discern the moment when adolescence arrives. Puberty is a biological stage; adolescence, middle age, and the rest are social classifications. A few years ago Kenneth Keniston decided that we needed a new category to describe characteristic human progress through the life cycle; he accordingly established, single-handed, a period which he called "youth," after adolescence, before adulthood. His addition hasn't yet won general acceptance, but it calls attention to the essential artifice of our chronological divisions.

"Artifice" is not, in this sense, a bad word. Only by means of artifice do we organize reality sufficiently to believe that we understand it, in life as in literature. The point may be made clearer through reflection on the earliest familiar statement of the view that the life cycle consists of separable periods: Jacques' speech in *As You Like It,* which begins with the assertion that "All the world's a stage, And all men and women merely players," and continues to explain that the "many parts" played by one man in his time divide themselves into acts of seven ages. The roles which Jacques describes as part of universal experience are delineated through occupation—the infant who mewls and pukes, the whining schoolboy, the lover, the soldier, and so on to the dotard who "ends...sans every thing." We may find an interesting chapter of social history in the particular sequence of occupations, but in the present context the most significant aspect of Jacques' list is its reliance on the metaphor of stage performance— familiar in many Renaissance accounts of human life, but here particularly revealing, I think, of the kind of artifice involved in considering life as a series of definable stages. To understand experience thus is to watch the self in the process of enacting its changes; to write an autobiography commits one to performing one's changing selfhood in public.

First we create the division of life; then we develop attitudes toward them. The perception that autobiographies in different historical periods imply different valuations of various stages in the life cycle emphasizes the fact that each era evolves its own pet attitudes. Yet renewed reflection on autobiographies generates the further perception that this diversity of emphasis conceals an identity of purpose: the eighteenth century found in the idea of "maturity" some of the same satisfactions that the twentieth century discovers in adolescence. Human beings seek always the loci of pleasure and power. They may expect to find these elusive rewards in one stage of life or another; their ways of centering such expectation imply their sense of the relation between themselves and their social contexts. But the modes of artifice involved in every instance speak of what all autobiographers—perhaps all human beings—hold in common. Colley Cibber in the eighteenth century as much as Norman Mailer in the twentieth sets out in his memoir (his *Apology,* he calls it) to perform himself. The role he chooses is that of competent citizen; Mailer prefers that of perpetually unreconciled adolescent. But both men through their chosen roles draw to themselves the power, claim for themselves the pleasure, which they value. And both also betray comparable senses of grievance.

A reader of the *Boston Globe* recently wrote to the solve-your-problems column with an inquiry about Colley Cibber. He had come across the name in a list of poets laureate; it sounded so improbable that he wished to know if any such person had in fact existed, and if so, what he had done or written. Cibber's accomplishments, duly rehearsed by the columnist, sound remarkably thin. He wrote many plays, but no one remembers them; he held the position of poet laureate, but everyone knew him as a dreadful poet; he wrote his autobiography. Even Dr. Johnson approved of that, but who reads it now? Actually it repays reading. The emphatic theatricality of Cibber's self-presentation underlines the note of belligerence which dominates his tone. Again like Mailer, he is professionally outrageous. When he announces that his muse and his wife were equally prolific, producing respectively a play and a child a year (an observation which particularly infuriated Pope), we may suspect him of wishing to be offensive; as he develops an argument that vanity, his ruling passion, accounts for most aspects of his character and for his success, suspicion yields to certainty. But the outrageousness, as he constantly reminds us, does not provide his fundamental principle of self-justification; *success* is in fact what justifies him. He tells many stories of failure—of his schoolfellows ostracizing him in his youth, of audiences refusing to applaud, women refusing to succumb—but in every instance, failure converts itself finally to its opposite. People believe he writes bad verses, but he has won the laureateship; people say he lacks the voice for tragedy, but he had made money as a theater manager; those who scorn him often return to ask his advice. What makes him interesting to himself and, he assumes, to other people is his achievement of notoriety and of prosperity in a capitalistic society.

Cibber is very much a special case in his own time; other people did not write the same sort of autobiography. But even at his extreme of what one might call childish self-display, one finds the century's characteristic stress on the accomplishments of adulthood as the measure of selfhood. To accept the time of life in which one is actually in the process of writing the autobiography as the period best defining identity implies a state of considerable reconciliation with the existent society, since emphasis on the present or recent past rather than on more distant times of life suggests a relative commitment to reality, to things-as-they-are, rather than to fantasy, which separates self from community. But Cibber's reconciliation, like that of his contemporaries, is far from complete.

The strain which attends the playing of a part (surely no one feels, no one has ever felt, like a grown-up all the time) emerges by indirection in the grievances reported or revealed by eighteenth-century self-describers. "Human life is everywhere a state in which there is much to be endured and little to be enjoyed," Dr. Johnson wrote; he did not write his autobiography. Those who did, formulate their awareness of life's hardships in terms of a personal drama of inadequate approval and help from others. Arthur Young's unhappy marriage provides the center of this drama in his account; Hume's experience of lack of appreciation focuses on negative reviews of his work; absence of applause supplies a central symbol for Cibber. But all, in stressing their worldly success, stress also the degree to which it represented a triumph over others—a competitive triumph, and an achievement in the face of lack of psychic support. The pose of adulthood, in other words, has its childish underside. If maturity represented the arena of power and pleasure, eighteenth-century writers about themselves also suggest their feeling that it never supplies enough of either. Their claim of social reconciliation amounts to a recognition that to live in society is the best they can do (although during this period, of course, people also began to speculate about what it might be like to exist without civilization)—but with considerable awareness that society generates its own discontents.

This intensifying awareness, in the next century, was exactly what helped to create the widespread nostalgia for childhood. The pleasure and power associated with childhood belong to the state of passivity and dependence, deriving as they do from the force exerted by those who can demand the care of others. To complain about childhood, as Spencer and (less openly) Mill do, is necessarily to complain about other people; to glorify childhood implies acceptance and even exaltation of others. To look upon childhood as life's high point equates irresponsibility with happiness. It may also suggest profound social pessimism, a hopelessness about the state of the world expressed in nostalgia for a time of life when no one could possibly expect one to do anything about it. DeQuincey's heroic vision of the self as infant in effect parodies the view conveyed by so many nineteenth-century autobiographies, that the being imagined as helpless can best be imagined as interesting. Even his or her unhappiness is interesting; and if childhood is the state of least social power, it is also that of most intense feeling. Glorifying the child version of self, then, enabled autobiographers to epitomize a complex system of values and assumptions.

In the light of these reflections, it becomes increasingly apparent that the twentieth-century preoccupation with adolescence cannot be dismissed simply as evidence of the superficiality or corruption of the modern world. To locate power and pleasure in this time of life suggests a kind of reconciliation between the eighteenth-century and the nineteenth-century view. The eighteenth-century assumption that only full social functioning could be admired yielded to the counter-view that such functioning involved so much compromise, so much pain, as to destroy capacity for feeling and particularly for happiness. We have by no means returned, in literary circles, to the opinion that worldly success measures worth and the possibility of fulfillment. On the other hand, in celebrating adolescence we celebrate the maximum potential for *imagining* the power of uncompromised activity in the world, for imagining even the chance of changing the world, if only to the extent of making one's personal position in it more comfortable.

The autobiographical records of members of minority groups, for whom the likelihood of affecting society often disappears in the hard struggles of everyday survival, emphasize this point by their own use of the material of adolescence. Anne Moody's *Coming of Age in Mississippi,* an account of a black girl's simultaneous discovery of sexual power and social powerlessness, achieves poignance by its constant implicit and explicit contrast between what the girl can imagine and what she can do. *The Autobiography of Malcolm X* dwells lovingly on the teenage years, although the adult writer explicitly rejects the values of his youthful self. At the age of seventeen, he achieved prosperity by selling marijuana in Harlem. "I felt, for the first time in my life," he summarizes, "that great feeling of *free!*" The sense of freedom, of course, rapidly yields to increasing awareness of entrapment and soon to literal imprisonment. Yet it represents a lifetime goal—a goal of insistent meaning to the black man, but one yearned for in various modes by everyone; and one which most people attain, or in retrospect believe themselves to have attained, only in adolescence.

A peculiarly expressive account of the imaginative meaning of the adolescent life stage is Maxine Hong Kingston's *The Woman Warrior,* an important autobiographical achievement not only for the sheer power of its writing but because of its skillful use of fantasy as part of the essential material of a life story. The narrator's Chinese mother spends much time in "story-talk"; the daughter is also a story-talker. Her central myth involves perceiving herself as savior of her people. To achieve heroism, she imagines, she must leave her family and go to live on a mountain with an old man and an old woman who carefully train her. Halfway through her stay on the mountain, she experiences her first menstruation; now, she is told, she can have children. "I bled and thought about the people to be killed," she observes; "I bled and thought about the people to be born." When she returns to her family as a warrior, she marries the man her parents have chosen for her, rides into battle with him, takes a single day off from fighting to give birth, and carries her infant boy inside her armor.

This vision of uniting the power of both sexes centers on the period of adolescent potential—the time of imagining, the time of training, of growth and of possibility. Like Adam and Eve, we find the world all before us at this juncture, cast out from the childhood paradise toward which our forefathers and mothers yearned, not yet chained to the circumspect realities which our more distant forefathers bravely glorified. Our vision of heroism is not De-Quincey's and not Benjamin Franklin's—although it has much in common with theirs. Visions of heroism are modes of dramaturgy. When one climbs upon a literary stage to perform the self, one chooses the costume, assumes the poses, that the audience of one's own time—and oneself as audience—will recognize.

Unsettling the Colonel's Hash:
"Fact" in Autobiography

by Darrel Mansell

"Artists in Uniform: A Story by Mary McCarthy" appeared in *Harper's Magazine* (March 1953). The piece describes an encounter in the club car of a train, and later in a station restaurant, between a woman and an anti-Semitic air force colonel. In 1954 McCarthy published an essay, "Settling the Colonel's Hash."[1] She discusses various questions, comments, and interpretations of "Artists in Uniform" passed on to her by readers, and goes on to give her own "idea" (p.237) of the work, its "chief moral or meaning" (p. 239) to her. Here is an author's sincere and genial attempt to set her readers right on what she meant. Such an attempt always raises fundamental issues concerning the nature of art, and below I want to explore one of them.

According to McCarthy, her readers have been misled from the beginning. For it was the editors of the magazine who were responsible for the subtitle that refers to "Artists in Uniform" as a "story." "I myself," she says, "would not know quite what to call it; it was a piece of reporting or a fragment of autobiography" (p. 226). Indeed, the

> whole point of this "story" was that it really happened; it is written in the first person; I speak of myself in my own name, McCarthy....
> When I was thinking about writing the story, I decided not to treat it fictionally; the chief interest, I felt, lay in the fact that it happened, in real life, ...to the writer herself.... (p. 227)

The fact that the events "happened, in real life" makes all the difference to her. For when her readers asked whether details like

"Unsettling the Colonel's Hash: 'Fact' in Autobiography" by Darrel Mansell, From *Modern Language Quarterly*, 37, no. 2 (June 1976), 115-32. Reprinted by permission of *Modern Language Quarterly* and the author.

[1]*Harper's Magazine*, February 1954, pp. 68-75. My quotations are from the version that appeared in McCarthy's *On the Contrary* (New York, 1961), pp. 225-41.

the colonel's having hash for lunch were "symbolic" of something in the same way such details might be symbolic in fiction ("a Eucharist or a cannibal feast or the banquet of Atreus" [p. 232]), she felt the correct response was to say that there "were no symbols in this story; there was no deeper level. The nuns were in the story because they were on the train;...the colonel had hash because he had hash..." (p. 229).

McCarthy is making the assumption we all make except in our stern philosophical moments: that there are two more or less separate literary kinds, "autobiography" and "narrative fiction"; and that these are separate because the one deals substantially with fact, what "happened, in real life," no matter how "artistic" the presentation, and the other deals substantially with what did not happen but was only "imagined," no matter how convincingly "real." Our "autobiography" and "fiction" categories thus seem themselves to be manifestations of an even more fundamental distinction, between declarations of "fact" and some other broad category of fictitious or otherwise imaginative works.

The distinction appears in Coleridge's *Biographia Literaria*: there is a "species of composition, which is opposed to works of science, by proposing for its *immediate* object pleasure, not truth",[2] and this general idea is absolutely crucial in modern literary theory. There is a Great Divide that runs down the center of the literary map. Works like autobiography which deal for the most part, with what we can suppose "happened, in real life"—these lie somewhere high on one slope that terminates in the smooth waters of pure scientific discourse. The various forms of "fiction" lie somewhere on the other slope, at the bottom of which is whatever one could conceive to be purely imaginative literature, "the foam/Of perilous seas, in faery lands forlorn." Thus René Wellek and Austin Warren distinguish between the "scientific uses of language" and the "literary" uses; Cleanth Brooks distinguishes between the "terms of science" and poetic language; Northrop Frye between "descriptive" writing and literature; I. A. Richards between the "undistorted references" of science and "*fictions*"; and in a recent article Ralph W. Rader refers typically to that "fundamental contrast between the fictional and the factual narrative modes."[3]

---

[2]Ed. J. Shawcross, 2 vols. (Oxford, 1907), II, 10.

[3]Wellek and Warren, *Theory of Literature* (New York, 1949), p. 11; Brooks, *The Well-Wrought Urn* (New York, 1947), p.210; Frye, *Anatomy of Criticism* (Princeton, 1957), p.74;

This distinction helps a librarian decide where to put *The Education of Henry Adams* and *David Copperfield*. The one book may not entirely conform to what we know of Adams's life, and the other may have drawn much of its material from Dickens's own. Still, one falls under "fact" and narrates events we suppose "happened" to some controlling degree; the other is on the opposite side of the Great Divide and narrates events we suppose are mostly imagined.

Granted, there are borderline cases. Is *Sartor Resartus* fiction, Carlyle's veiled autobiography, or perhaps something else?[4] But we can, and do, solve such problems by turning them into a simple matter of proportion. We tote up the specific details that seem fictional (the hero's name, Teufelsdröckh) and the ones that seem factual (Carlyle said elsewhere that his character's spiritual conversion resembled his own), and decide to our own satisfaction which predominates. We still end up making a pretty and uncomplicated distinction. As Frye puts it, "an autobiography coming into a library would be classified as nonfiction if the librarian believed the author, and as fiction if she thought he was lying" (p. 303).

Thus that fundamental critical distinction between statements of truth and fiction has always put autobiography on one side of the Divide, and almost everything we think of as "literature" on the other. Autobiography becomes a species of scientific discourse—and indeed the Library of Congress classification system makes Autobiography a subclass of Biography, and Biography a subclass of the "Auxiliary Sciences of History."[5] Likewise, Wayne Shumaker makes autobiography, along with biography and history, one of the "factural literary types"; Barrett J. Mandel lists "avowed truth" as one of the features that set autobiography off from other kinds of literature; and Käte Hamburger makes the general statement that "an innate characteristic of every first-person narrative" is that "it posits itself as non-fic-

---

Richards, *Principles of Literary Criticism* (New York, 1924), p. 266; Rader, "Literary Form in Factural Narrative: The Example of Boswell's *Johnson*," in *Essays in Eighteenth-Century Biography*, ed. Philip B. Daghlian (Bloomington, 1968), p. 3.

[4]Frye uses this example (p. 303). I note that the bibliography in Roy Pascal's *Design and Truth in Autobiography* (Cambridge, Mass., 1960) lists Somerset Maugham's *Of Human Bondage* as an autobiography; Maugham himself called it an "autobiographical novel" (*The Summing Up* [London, 1938], p. 196); the Library of Congress system classifies it as fiction (PR).

[5]See John Phillip Immroth, *A Guide to Library of Congress Classification* (Rochester, 1968), p. 180.

tion, i.e., as a historical document," a "reality statement."[6] So, we think
of autobiography as a more or less direct relation of factual truth;
and we even pass judgement on autobiographies according to whether they stick to the facts, the way things "happened, in real life."
Roy Pascal, for instance, points out that when we read an autobiography, "We like to ask, does the author's representation of himself...
correspond to what we can get to know of him through other evidence? It is a question that can never be asked regarding a work of
art" (p. 188).

Autobiography therefore is not "art," not "literature," not "fiction."
It is on the side of biography, history, and the truth-telling sciences.
Its truth is occasionally conceived as somehow "higher" than a mere
conscientious relation of fact;[7] but there is absolutely no way to free
autobiography significantly from its obligation to fact. Here we are at
the core of what seems to differentiate this genre from "fiction." We
really do believe that autobiography is somehow obligated to fact,
what happened in real life, in a way that "literature" is not. We believe
that fact is fact, and fiction is something else. We have not progressed
far beyond that simple, inexpugnable distinction Sir Philip Sidney
took for granted long ago: "Think I none so simple would say the
Esope lyed in the tales of his beasts: for who thinks that *Esope* writ
it for actually true were well worthy to haue his name cronicled
among the beastes hee writeth of."[8]

But what happens when we examine this distinction, not as a belief,
but as a critical, or aesthetic, or even "philosophical" principle for
separating autobiography from fiction? The principle erodes, until
there is nothing left.

[6]Shumaker, *English Autobiography* (Berkeley, 1954), p. 101; Mandel, "The Autobiographer's Art," *JAAC*, 27 (1968), 219; Hamburger, *The Logic of Literature*, trans,
Marilynn J. Rose, 2nd ed. (Bloomington, 1973), pp. 312, 328-29.

[7]Following is a sampler of statements to this effect, none of them easily comprehensible. Georg Misch, *A History of Autobiography in Antiquity*, 2 vols. (London, 1950),
I, II: "in general, the spirit brooding over the recollected material is the truest and
most real element in an autobiography." Georges Gusdorf, "Conditions et limites de
l'autobiographie," in *Formen der Selbstdarstellung*, ed. Günter Reichenkron and Erich
Haase (Berlin, 1956): "l'autobiographie est une seconde lecture de I expérience, et
plus vraie que la première, puisqu'elle en est la prise de conscience" (p. 114); "dans le
cas de l'autobiographie, la vérité des faits apparaît subordonnée à la vérité de
l'homme..." (p. 118).

[8]*"An apology for Poetry,"* in *Elizabethan Critical Essays*, ed. G. Gregory Smith, 2 vols.
(1904; rpt. London, 1964), I, 185.

To begin with, how do we decide whether to take something as fact or fiction? Suppose somebody writes on a piece of paper, "I was born on a Friday, at twelve o'clock at night." Fact or fiction? There is of course no way of telling (in this case it is Dickens's David Copperfield speaking).[9] But why not? Perhaps our first impulse is to say, "Because we do not know who 'I' is and therefore have no way of verifying whether what he said did actually happen in real life."

It turns out, however, that this has little to do with how we actually make up our minds. We hardly ever have any independent means (history books, private records, and so on) of verifying what a man writes. More important, even our sense of whether his statements have "probability" on their side or not—even this, while it obviously makes a considerable difference to us, can never serve as an absolute distinction between truth-telling discourse, such as autobiography, and fictional discourse, such as a novel.

In the *Apologia Pro Vita Sua*, for example, there is a famous passage in which Newman, visiting Italy, begins to think he has a mission in life. An acquaintance urges him to visit Rome, but he replies

> with great gravity, "We have a work to do in England." I went down at once to Sicily, and the presentiment grew stronger. I struck into the middle of the island, and fell ill of a fever at Leonforte. My servant thought that I was dying, and begged for my last directions. I gave them, as he wished; but I said, "I shall not die." I repeated, "I shall not die, for I have not sinned against light, I have not sinned against light."[10]

After many tribulations, including being becalmed on an orange boat in the Straits of Bonifacio, he reaches his mother's house in England within hours of his brother's return from Persia and within five days of the great Assize Sermon that he later considers to have begun the Oxford Movement.

Here is an autobiographical passage that is apt to strike some readers (especially non-Catholic ones) as less "probable," more likely to have been shaped significantly by the author's purposeful imagination,[11] than almost anything in the highly probable and realistic *Robinson Crusoe*. "Probability" would therefore not work very well in the

[9]Chapter 1 of *David Copperfield*, edited for my own purposes.

[10]John Henry Newman, *Apologia Pro Vita Sua*, ed. Martin J. Svaglic (Oxford, 1967), p. 43.

[11]George Levine, *The Boundaries of Fiction* (Princeton, 1968), pp. 246-50, makes much the same point about this passage.

case of this one event if we wanted to decide whether the work it comes from were autobiography or fiction.

One might suppose that the examples above are too short, and have been unfairly lifted out of context, and that if we only had long enough passages it would be easy enough to decide whether a work is relating events likely or not to have happened in real life. "Probability" therefore still would work as a means of discriminating autobiography from fiction. This seems to make sense, for when we have a whole book in our hands we almost always know immediately whether we are to take it as autobiography or fiction (or something else); and we might be inclined to think the reason for this is that there is some larger "context" of words that does the trick even when short and perverse excerpts like the ones above do not.

Occasionally something like this does occur. We get a sense of an aggregate probability built up word by word to make some large context that is saying "this book must be true" (or "fiction," or whatever)—one of those rare cases where we actually decide what genre a book belongs to as we go along. Much more often, however, the "probability" of the text has little or nothing to do with how we "take" a book. We decide on other grounds. A friend's or a critic's comment, or the library shelf, or the title page specifies a genre—specifies whether we are to take the book "as true" or not.

In the course of reading *David Copperfield* or the *Apologia*, for instance, no one decides whether the work is fiction or autobiography; he was "given" that before he began. In these cases we are not so much gathering a sense of probability *from* the text as engaging in a mental act that comes close to conferring a sense of probability *on* the text: that is, we have been told to make a certain assumption, and we therefore make it and are willing to persist in it even when a novelist says in the first person something temptingly like autobiography, or an autobiographer something suspiciously like fiction.[12] Thus a scheme for extracting sunbeams from cucumbers is perhaps a little less probable for being in a book titled *Gulliver's Travels* (bk. 3, chap. 5) than it might be in a histology journal. Even large contexts of "probability" in a work seldom, therefore, play much of a part in our decision whether to take the work "as true"; we usually have our

---

[12]For a discussion of how we stubbornly make the details of a text conform to our preconceived idea of the genre of the text, see E.D. Hirsch, Jr., *Validity in Interpretation* (New Haven, 1967), pp. 164-69. "It is very difficult to dislodge or relinquish one's own genre idea, since that idea seems so totally adequate to the text" (p. 166).

minds made up for us at the start, and to some degree we give the author's "probabilities" the benefit of the doubt.[13]

What gives us this initial idea of the work? There are all sorts of answers, as we have seen. But here we come to the crucial point: for no matter how we got whatever impression we have of whether we ought to take the book "as true" or not—this of course says nothing about whether the book *is* "true." If the author himself, or the card catalogue, or something else gives us a sense that the book is to be considered as relating events that did really happen in life, we still know nothing about the actual relation of the book to the "world."

What we do know is a supposed relation of the book to the author himself. That is, we almost never know the actual relation of literary events to what "happened, in real life," and on that basis decide whether we are reading fiction or autobiography; but we *do* know, or think we know, what the author *intends* the relation to be. We know that somebody (in McCarthy's case, apparently an editor at *Harper's*) is positing a relationship, such as "the author intends his work to be taken as fiction," or as "what really happened." The established assumption of what the author intends—that is everything.

The large-scale probability, the verisimilitude, of what an author says in his book therefore has to be considered merely a rhetorical strategy, like the title page and all sorts of other tricks of the trade, to establish an intended genre for his work. The actual relation of the work to reality is problematical, and nothing more. Indeed, there is no reason why an autobiographer could not use some plausible event that never actually happened to help "declare" his work autobiographical; no reason why he should not reject an unbelievable event that *did* happen for fear of damaging his declaration; no reason why a novelist could not use that same event to help establish his own work as fiction.[14]

[13]There is a similar comment of Ludwig Wittgenstein's on the difference "context" makes: "I describe a psychological experiment: the apparatus, the questions of the experimenter, the actions and replies of the subject—and then I say that it is a scene in a play.—Now everything is different" (*Philosophical Investigations*, trans. G.E.M. Ansombe, 2nd ed. [New York, 1958], p. 180e).

[14]But Newman makes an interesting comment on this: "Miss Edgeworth sometimes apologizes for certain incident [*sic*] in her tales, by stating they took place 'by one of those strange chances which occur in life, but seem incredible when found in writing.' Such an excuse evinces a misconception of the principle of fiction, which, being the perfection of the actual, prohibits the introduction of any such anomalies of experience" ("Poetry, with Reference to Aristotle's Poetics," *Essays Critical and Historical* [London, 1901], I, 13-14).

Therefore we have to concede at least in theory that absolutely anything a writer says can be "taken" as true or false if his declared or inferred intention is that we should do so. Whether or not David Copperfield's birth "happened, in real life" is irrelevant; we take it as fiction because we got an impression, in this case largely by means that have nothing to do with the "probability" of the text itself, of the author's intention ("*The Personal History, Adventures, Experiences, & Observations of David Copperfield The Younger of Blunderstone Rookery [Which He never meant to be Published on any Account]*"). The same would hold for a statement even if we had a sneaking suspicion it was a lie (such as a man's account of how he first appeared to his parents in a "green-silk Basket, such as neither Imagination nor authentic Spirits are wont to carry"), or a statement obviously a lie (such as the miraculous birth of Gargantua through the left ear of his mother).[15]

If the author or somebody else were to communicate to us, in some way we thought superseded what we could gather from the probability of these statements themselves, that we were to take them as true, we would have no choice but to try—no matter how much that taxed our credulity or patience. Our own appraisal of whether the statement is indeed true would present a problem: we would be likely to think that a man who sincerely claimed such things were autobiographical was either demented or insulting our intelligence. But in both cases the man would still be writing his autobiography no matter how pathetic or preposterous we were to consider him, and it.

The conclusion to be drawn reluctantly from this is that when we are determining which side of the great fact-fiction watershed a book belongs on, its conforming or not conforming to the facts of reality is irrelevant. We make our determination on the basis of the author's declared or inferred intention, and the probability or plausibility of what he says is merely one of many means at his disposal for establishing his intention. The genre "autobiography" seems therefore a matter of the author's intention, nothing more. As Shumaker puts it, the "determining consideration" is the "autobiographical intention." If the author "wishes to be understood as writing of himself and as setting down (so far as is humanly possible) nothing that is

[15]The first example is the arrival of the baby Teufelsdröckh. *Sartor Resartus*, bk. 2, chap. I; the second, *Gargantua*, bk. I, chap. 6.

not literally and factually true, his work is autobiography. ... If he wishes to be understood as writing imaginatively, it is something else" (p. 105).[16]

Thus the crucial distinction between "autobiography" and "fiction" is not to be found by comparing what a man writes to the "world outside"; the distinction seems to exist inside the writer's own head. So we now move from "outer" to "inner" matters. To begin with, what would make a writer decide to call his work autobiography, or fiction? Again, the answer seems simple. The writer, more than anybody else, is able to declare his writing one or the other on the basis of whether or not what he writes "happened, in real life."

But what does it mean to say that a related event (say, a man's eating hash for lunch) "happened, in real life"? Certainly not that the putative event got transferred into words. The event was, or occurred in, a mass existing in space and time; and all that words can do is make reference to such matters. So, obvious as it is, we have to let go at once of the comfortable idea that related events "happened."

Then the related words are a simulacrum, a verbal rendition, of the event. But what does that mean? Certainly not that the words somehow reproduce the entirety of the event. If McCarthy were to reproduce the top of the colonel's luncheon plate, there is still the hidden bottom, and also the hidden genealogy of the hash and the colonel. The autobiographer's words, like the novelist's and everybody else's, must artificially delimit, and therefore distort, the event. "Every limit is a beginning as well as an ending," as we are told in the last chapter of George Eliot's *Middlemarch.*

Thus related events have not "happened, in real life." The autobiographer, like every other relator of events fictive or "real," is engaged in a process of purposeful selection. "Autobiography means... selection in face of the endless complexity of life, selection of facts, distribution of emphases, choice of expression" (Pascal, p. 10).[17] In this respect an autobiographer is no different (except perhaps in degree?) from any other artist: he selects from what is somehow before him. A man "with absolutely truthful intention, amid the multitude of facts presented to him must needs select, and in selecting assert

---

[16]I have edited a (minor?) proviso out of the quotation.
[17]Mandel makes the same point (p. 218).

something of his own humour, something that comes not of the world without but of a vision within."[18] So a man who chose to call his work autobiography or fiction solely on the basis of whether or not he made a purposeful selection from what he could have "put in" would be deluding somebody—himself or us.

Furthermore, the autobiographer, like the novelist, is apt to change the bits of reality he selects, and thus to fictionalize them. "Il faut changer la vie," as he knows.[19] Sometimes this happens without his knowing it. Like the rest of us, he has his quirks, anxieties, and mental defenses. He is on especially dangerous ground when, like McCarthy, he professes and apparently believes he is telling the truth. Such a grand purpose "has only to be proclaimed for it to become questionable. We know only too much about the inner censor, that acts so perfidiously because it acts automatically" (Pascal, p. 61).

But usually autobiographers know perfectly well what they are doing: like novelists, they are selecting and altering personal experience so as to create a structure of words that answers to an inner vision or purpose of some kind. As James Olney, the author of a fine, modern study of autobiography, notes: "One creates from moment to moment and continuously the reality to which one gives a metaphoric name and shape, and that shape is one's own shape."[20] McCarthy can claim that the details in "Artists in Uniform" are there because they "happened," but that cannot quite be the case. To say that a detail appears *because* it happened is not the same as saying it *did* happen. She says the former (p. 229) but must mean the latter. For there must have been other details that did happen during the experience but do not appear in the piece. Why are they absent?

Probably because they contributed nothing to, or even detracted from, the author's own sense of what her work ought to be like, a sense that could only be communicated, to the extent it could be communicated at all, by the details she chose (and created?). As for those absent details (the colonel's name, for instance), is it somehow untruthful to the event that they are absent? Certainly not. Because what the—shall we call it a story?—is being "true" to is not real life, but a conception an artist has derived from life, a conception

---

[18]Walter Pater, "Style," *Appreciations*, in *Works*, New Library Ed., 10 vols. (London 1910), V, 9.

[19]Michel Butor, "Une Autobiographie dialectique," *Répertoire*, I (Paris, 1960), 262.

[20]*Metaphore of Self: The Meaning of Autobiography* (Princeton, 1972), p. 34. Pascal makes a similar comment (p. 72).

that apparently got its initial impulse from life and then shaped itself as the writer began to cull from the experience (and alter, and create?) the details that would be the most adequate literary expression of that constantly changing conception (McCarthy comments on this herself, pp. 240-41).

Furthermore, the autobiographer, in trying to make his material answer to his vision, his purpose, his conception, is likely to be influenced by the demands of formal "conventions," there are "patterns" in autobiography.[21] "What one seeks in reading autobiography is not a date, a name, or a place, but a characteristic way of perceiving, of organizing..." (Olney, p. 37). The main (but not the only) strength of autobiography, like the main strength of all literature, is internal, in its "form," rather than in any correspondence to "fact," to "truth," to "what happened." The autobiographer therefore makes, in very general terms, the same kinds of aesthetic decisions, resulting in the same kind of aesthetic product, as any other literary artist. Indeed, we had better "speak of autobiography in the language of 'formal' literary criticism..." (Mandel, p. 218).[22]

So it seems that there is no reason for calling something "autobiography" that could not also be a reason for calling it "fiction." There is no way an author or anybody else could make a distinction between autobiography and fiction that would not crumble in his hands. There is nothing decisive in the relation of words to what happened. nothing decisive in the writer's own mental processes, nothing decisive in the organization of the words on the page—nothing that makes an essential distinction between the two kinds of writing. Regarded aesthetically, critically, "philosophically," the distinction so handy and familiar to us all breaks down. This is outrageous to common sense. But it seems an inexorable critical principle.

There is a saying, "Every artist writes his own autobiography"[23]— a saying that certainly seems borne out when a man in the preface to his own declared autobiography apologizes for the fact that some of the material has already appeared in his novels.[24] Why not leave

[21]See Pascal, p. 2; Levine, p. 170: "One of the distinctive characteristics of autobiography...is the imposition of a pattern. ..."

[22]Gusdorf also has a relevant comment: "il faut donc admettre une sorte de renversement de perspective, et renoncer à considérer l'autobiographie à la manière d'une biographie objective, régie par les seules exigences du genre historique. Toute autobiographic est une oeuvre d'art..." (p. 120).

[23]Cited by H. N. Wethered, *The Curious Art of Autobiography* (London, 1956), p. 2.

[24]Nikolai Gubsky, *Angry Dust: An Autobiography* (New York, 1937), p. ix.

it at that? All one's imaginative life is derived somehow from personal experience; all writing by some process of indirection "happened" — even magic casements in faery lands forlorn, "There is no Arte deliuered to mankinde that hath not the workes of Nature for his principall object..." (Sidney, p. 155). And likewise any account of what happened is bound to be colored by the imaginative life of the person telling the story. If we can accept all this, "autobiography" and "fiction" are—both autobiography and fiction; and we can look with pefect equanimity on the following title appearing in the "fiction" section of a recent magazine: "*Fredi & Shirl & the Kids: The Autobiography in Fables of Richard M. Elman*, A Novel, by Richard Elman."[25]

But no matter how much we question the rationale of distinguishing between "autobiography" and "fiction," no matter how thoroughly we convince ourselves that there is no essential difference between the two, the distinction does get made. Somehow an "intention" declares itself to us. So finally we must ask ourselves: what difference should that declared intention make in how we read the book?

McCarthy seems to be claiming it should make all the difference in the world. To the question, "What is the colonel's hash symbolic of?" she answers, "Symbolic of nothing, because what I wrote (*pace* my editors) is not fiction but autobiography." This seems to mean that a detail like the colonel's hash is potentially "symbolic" (in McCarthy's literary sense of referring to some idea beyond itself) or not symbolic according to whether the detail appears in something declared fiction or something declared autobiography. Does that make sense?

At first sight it does. If we get the idea that words on a page are an account of "what happened," we tend to assume with McCarthy that the related details are arrested in something like a literal stage; we assume that hash "means" simply hash. We assume that the details which exist in the work do so primarily, and probably exclusively, because they existed in a reality that is being recorded. Further inquiries into their "literary" meaning, inquiries into what ideas the details might have been contrived to "stand for" beyond themselves, seem almost, if not entirely, stultified. When Newman in the *Apologia*

[25]The equanimity of the reviewer was a little less than perfect: "The first question this book raises is whether the 'Richard Elman' given as the author is any different from the 'Richard M. Elman' in the subtitle..."(*New Yorker*, August 5, 1972, p. 82).

refers to the "orange boat" that carried him away from Sicily en route to his great work in England, not many readers (but see note 11) would want to look for any further significance whatever in this beyond its intrisic interest as a vivid detail carried over from life.

But surely this attitude is irrational. Can we really put faith in whatever we can find out about an author's supposed state of mind at the time she wrote—whatever it is she now says she wrote? If she seems to recall that the events in her work somehow derived from what she remembers as "life" to an extent that, even considering omissions, revisions, and other transmogrifications, she now for whatever reason considers significant, does any declaration of this cut off the possibility of the kinds of symbolic meaning there would be if the work had somehow got itself classified as "fiction"?

Are we supposed to believe that the word "hash" on a page of *Harper's* has potentially a symbolic meaning for about a year, then changes and no longer has that potential meaning because the author (or suppose someone else) wrote in a book or a letter or whispered to a friend that she remembers there existed real hash on a plate that she now identifies with the words "corned-beef hash" on page 47 of the March 1953 *Harper's*? Was there anything else on the real colonel's plate, a pickled pear omitted in the story but existing in reality, so that McCarthy is now in the state of reporting real hash that happened on an otherwise fictive plate? Can the rest of the plate be "symbolic" but not the hash? What if the station restaurant reports in and says it was lamb hash—can we go back then to symbolizing the word in the story? In *David Copperfield* should we fence off whatever details seem to have a more direct relation than the others to Dickens's own life, and not consider them as "literature"?

In short, should a work have a different status, a different ontology as an artifact, according to somebody's declared guess concerning the relation of "what happened" to words on a page? Can there be any reasonable answer but No?

In the archangel Michael's words to Adam, "Let us descend now therefore from this top / Of Speculation." Suppose we are convinced to our satisfaction (or, even better, to our dissatisfaction) that there are no grounds for an essential distinction between autobiography and fiction. Nevertheless, the two genres do exist, and we are always encountering and relying on the distinction.

How is it that we can convince ourselves there is nothing intrinsic

in works that allows us to make an absolute distinction between
"fact" and "fiction," yet use the absolute distinction all the time?
The answer lies in the constitution of the mind. Any discrete thing
external to the mind can be perceived as a *Ding an sich*, or it can
be perceived "referentially," as referring to something beyond itself.
It can be taken to refer only to itself, to "be," no matter how tempting
its relation to a context beyond it; or it can be taken to refer to
some context outside itself, no matter how oblique or stylized the
reference. This is true of both a soup can and a book. We can regard
either as a self-referential object, hence "aesthetically," as "art." And
we can regard either as a referent, a "sign" referring to, and hence
making some kind of "statement" about, a context outside itself:
"Open me and there is something to eat"; "Open me and see what
happened, in real life."

There is no way of breaking down this distinction, although a
formulation that takes into account the obvious complexities is not
easy to arrive at. A piece of sculpture can have "reference," and can
even be conceived as making a statement useful in our lives; and a
useful object like a can or a hammer may have "beauty." But that is
merely a way of saying we can be "aware" of the mode of apprehension
we are not committed to, and may even have been committed to it
rather than the other a moment ago. Indeed, we are always aware
at least faintly of the possibility of apprehending a thing the other
way, the "truth" of statues and the "beauty" of hammers being a
tension between whichever mode we commit ourselves to and the
attractive possibilities of the other. In a context similar to mine,
Edmund Husserl refers to this tension as "perceptual consciousness
resolved in conflict."[26]

But the distinction itself is absolute, as Husserl emphasizes. An
arrow has got to point in a direction. A thing has got to be conceived
either as referring or not referring: referring outward or inward.
To imagine both at once is actually to imagine one followed by
the other. There is no mentally tenable third mode that combines
the two: "Take this thing as making a statement about 'life' but
as merely existing without making any such statement." Hence

[26]*Logical Investigations*, trans. J.N. Findlay, 2 vols. (London, 1970), II, 610. "Two
perceptual interpretations...of a thing interpenetrate.... And they interpenetrate in
conflicting fashion, so that our observation wanders from one to another...each
barring the other from existence" (II, 610).

"truth" and "beauty" always seem to fall into some kind of dialectical relationship.

Therefore that Great Divide between "fact" and "fiction" does not exist on the literary map at all; surely one can demonstrate that it does not. But such a Divide does exist nevertheless, in the very consitution of the mind, no matter what the mind is contemplating. Whether or not there is any absolute distinction in "kind" between a soup can and a Brancusi, between directions on an aspirin bottle and the *Apologia*, there is an absolute distinction between the two ways the mind can contemplate whatever is before it. Thus in the very constitution of the mind we have the rudiments of genre. All texts tend to be a conflation of fact and fiction. But the intending or inferring mind has *got* to declare for one or the other in spite of the unimpeachable truth that such a distinction does not "exist" in the texts themselves.

What we have now is a continuum of texts, concerning which the author's or somebody else's mind has made a reductive, artificial distinction: "Regardless of what this really is, consider it fact (or fiction)." Indeed, the various kinds of printed words arrange themselves in a shape like a horseshoe magnet. At one pole are texts such as the word "PUSH" on a door. Here the sign-maker's "intention" (probably gathered from the "context," a door) declares unambiguously that the sign be considered as "fact," as a reference to a state of affairs concerning how to open the door. A man would be hard put to conceive the sign "aesthetically" (for its onomatopoeia?).

We now move up the magnet away from the pole, through more and more complex organizations of "signs" that nevertheless manage to declare themselves "referential" (directions on an aspirin bottle, an article in a physics journal, and a history journal), until we get to texts like Darwin's account of the voyage of the *Beagle* and Gibbon's *Decline and Fall*. About here, about the place where we begin to talk about science and history books as having "style," our two modes begin to generate a little tension between themselves. The books are still managing to declare themselves "referential," but we begin to think that with a little perverseness of will we might change our apprehension to the aesthetic mode—and think of Darwin's ship as similar to Coleridge's in "The Rime of the Ancient Mariner."

Move a little further along the curve of the magnet and we are in a middle area (what would be the handle of the magnet) where the "intention" becomes more and more problematical, where apprehending the work in the mode of "truth" seems more or less balanced by the possibility of apprehending it in the mode of "beauty." Somewhere in this area, close to the center of the handle, we come to autobiography. Hence the problem, what is its intention, how are we to "take" it: as reference, as a type of history (the Library of Congress solution); or as "art," in which case we try to block out reference and to experience the work as poetry or fiction. Just to one side of center would probably be an autobiography like Newman's *Apologia*, where the context, the "intention," seems to be telling us to read for "what happened" (but presented with what style, what artistic purposefulness!); but where the context, the intention, seems also to be telling us that we *could* take the whole book aesthetically, as "fiction" (but with what truth to the author's own life!).

To the other side of center would be *Sartor Resartus*. As we move down this arm of the magnet, the tension between the two modes gradually relaxes the other way. We approach the "fiction" shelf in the library, which unambiguously declares for the aesthetic mode. Then poetry, which may have its theoretical terminus in whatever esoteric imagism one could imagine where the words, those signs pointing toward the world, have been so transformed by context, so bent inward, that external reference could be conceived as minimal. We are now in those faery lands forlorn, where it is far from easy to find aspirin-bottle "statements," cryptograms in the trees, sermons in stones. A little further and we approach the other *ultima Thule*, where direct external "reference" has (almost?) been locked out, and meaning is created solely by nonverbal signs moving about in a closed, self-referential context—mathematics. Thus "PUSH" and "$x = \frac{1}{2}(e^x + e^{-x})$" are poles apart, and in the precision and absoluteness of their mode of reference almost touching. Extremes meet.

Now, imagine an ideally "referential" mind confronted with our magnet. Such a mind would be comfortable at the "PUSH" pole and would be under increasing tension as it traveled toward the handle and the other pole. This mind would read Darwin's voyage for "truth," what happened, but would also be committed to reading *David Copperfield* as much as possible the same way (for moral apothegms that refer to life? for what "happened" to Dickens?). Likewise Coleridge's poem (for a moral, like "He prayeth best, who loveth best/ All things both great and small"? for what happened to a real mariner? or to Coleridge?), and likewise the hyperbolic cosine of x (here the mind boggles: a symbolic "statement" to apply to one's life? a symbolic analogue of real events?).

There is of course no such ideally "referential" mind. But as for an ideally "aesthetic" one—enter the critic. To him as critic everything from doorsigns and soup cans to cosines is to be apprehended in the "aesthetic" mode, and thus framed in a way that holds off any direct reference to life. Put more delicately, he has to see how the "sign" does indeed "refer" to reality in the act of deviating from it in whatever way allows an aesthetic apprehension (otherwise the "art" would collapse back into the real it "imitates"); but his awareness of reference is supposed to remain suspended in that precarious state. This, regardless of what the sign really "is," regardless of which intention it seems to be declaring for itself, or which of the two modes he would personally like to bring to bear on it. He may personally want to find the cloakroom, or be hungry, or be curious about Dickens's personal life; but to him as a critic all signs must be aesthetic signs.

To him as a critic a soup can is art. The can is now "like" a real can, but is an aesthetic object; he is not supposed to want to eat the contents, or judge the art according to whether he likes black bean more than asparagus. Likewise, he reads Coleridge's poem and knows that the ship is like a real ship (otherwise it could not be given the name) but is a poetic ship; it is not supposed to matter much to him as a critic whether the ship really existed, whether the adventures on it "happened, in real life."

And so to the critic as critic, all organizations of words are fiction! Fiction in its various forms. He looks in the glossary of *Anatomy of Criticism* and finds that "fiction" is another word for printed literature.[27] He finds nothing disturbing in this. He reads a first-aid manual "aesthetically," as "fiction," keeping his awareness of "reference" in that suspended state, and concentrating on structure, imagery, style.[28] He does the same with Dickens—and Henry Adams.

Yes, he reads autobiography as fiction. As for the *Apologia*, it "begins in the practical world and ends, as it were, framed like a

[27]See also Frye, p. 303; and R.G. Collingwood, *The Principles of Art* (Oxford, 1950), p. 285.

[28]See the critic Geoffrey Tillotson at work on a paragraph titled "Fainting," in "Matthew Arnold's Prose: Theory and Practice," in *The Art of Victorian Prose*, ed. George Levine and William Madden (New York, 1968), pp. 75-76.

novel. ... It survives as literature because it can sustain the contemplative and unpragmatic reading." Likewise, "anyone who attempts to teach Mill's *Autobiography*...quickly realizes that he is engaged in discussing a response to experience that differs very little if at all from the kind of thing he has been accustomed to think of as the peculiar activity of poets and novelists."[29]

The critic tries to assume that over every autobiography is hung a sign that says, "The opinions expressed here are not necessarily those of the management." If McCarthy says that the hash on the page corresponds to real hash in a restaurant, the critic does not care— or tries not to. To him *hash* is a word in an ultimately self-referring structure of words, and is therefore as potentially "symbolic" as any other word in that structure. Where the words came from does not matter; what to make of them is strictly his business, not McCarthy's. The job he took on when he dedicated himself to the aesthetic apprehension rather than the other was to try to see autobiography and everything else as cut off from any direct reference to what happened, in real life. "The secret to experiencing non-fiction prose as art lies not in the text but in ourselves: to the degree we can turn off our normal reality-testing, we can be drawn into non-fiction as a literary experience like our experience of poetry or fiction."[30]

That makes autobiography a special problem for him. Nobody ever expects him to read a doorsign or Darwin in a state of mind that suspends his awareness of reference; but autobiography, especially in recent years, is at least visible on his horizon. This taxes his aesthetic apprehension to the limit, for, as we have seen, autobiography exists in that area of our conceptual model where the possibilities of the two modes of apprehension are about balanced. Hence an area where words can be read either way, where "symbols" can be conceived as pointing either outward or inward (or outward-then-inward).

But not both ways at once. A crude and arbitary decision has *got* to be made; and the critic has opted for beauty. Thus when he reads autobiography he cuts himself off from "reference" he knows is there, but that cannot be the final issue of his thoughts. He has this problem with all texts to some extent' but he has the problem more in the case of autobiography than any other work with which

[29]Introduction to *The Art of Victorian Prose*, pp. xix, vii.
[30]Norman Holland, "Prose and Minds: A Psychoanalytic Approach to Non-Fiction," in *The Art of Victorian Prose*, p. 322.

he habitually deals. All texts are fact and fiction, but autobiography most of all. Hence his mind is under great tension. Can he ignore the potential truth of autobiography? Can he suspend his "reality-testing"? Can he resist reading the sign but not opening the door? Can he resist reading Newman for "what happened"? That is why, for criticism as a discipline, autobiography will always be a problem, and why the question of the colonel's hash can be settled theoretically —but never quite be settled.

Walden and the Temporal Mode of Autobiographical Narrative

by Janet Varner Gunn

> The earth is not a mere fragment of dead history, stratum upon stratum like the leaves of a book, to be studied by geologists and antiquaries chiefly, but living poetry like the trees, which precede flowers and fruit—not a fossil earth, but a living earth. ...

Until the day before yesterday, autobiography was looked on, if noticed at all, as "the dark continent of literature."[1] Its territory is under intense exploration today, much of it seemingly colonized and carved up into more easily managed subdivisions like the diary, the memoir, the confession, and what others would call "true" autobiography. Earlier a victim of benign neglect, autobiography seems now a victim of the taxonomical imperative—an imperative that serves more often to control the autobiographic genre than to understand its unruly behavior.

So firm a standing does the genre currently enjoy that it is even being deconstructed. No sooner has autobiography been certified a *bona fide* genre and worthy, therefore, of serious literary attention than it is now declared a hoax, or defined as though a mausoleum preserving a "self" which otherwise would not exist at all. As for its miragelike status, autobiography is viewed as but an illusory appearance of selfhood which masks the reality of a True Self that exists

"*Walden* and the Temporal Mode of Autobiographical Narrative," by Janet Varner Gunn. This is a substantially rewritten version of an essay which originally appeared in *Soundings: An Interdisciplinary Journal*, 60, no. 2 (Summer 1977), 194-209. Copyright 1977 by the Society for Values in Higher Education and Vanderbilt University.

[1]Stephen A. Shapiro, "The Dark Continent of Literature: Autobiography," *Comparative Literature Studies* 5 (December 1968), 421-54.

somewhere else. As one critic has recently put it, the "I" of autobiography is simply a "'dummy' ego"—a kind of Charlie McCarthy whose voice and movement are produced from some other location.[2] Autobiography, according to this Bergsonian argument, can be no more than a failed version of the autobiographer's real self, which is presumed buried under its various and changing appearances and therefore ineffable. The self cannot be put into words since, in Hemingway parlance, to say it is to lose it. Or in the terms I will be using, to convert the lived past into the presentness of language is, according to this view, to sacrifice *depth* to mere *surface*.

The other view of autobiography rests on a very different set of assumptions. While the proto-Platonists argue that language distorts and trivializes the self, the antimetaphysicians deny the self any status whatsoever outside of language. The "self-writing" cannot find its way into the text; the "self-written" cannot exist outside of it.[3]

Despite their differing assumptions about the relation of self and language, both views place on autobiography a "demand of total explicitness" which refuses any middle ground between presence and absence, allowing no place for the "lurking opacity behind what can be clearly formulated."[4] What this demand requires is not that the autobiographer-qua-Rousseau tell all, but that the remembered past and the anticipated future be superintended by an absolute present: in other words, that the life that has been and is even now being lived (in the act of writing it) be presented, as it were, on a single line, timeless yet immediate.

Neither view leaves room for what I take to be the human, and even religious, significance of autobiography, since both cut out of it the very heart of its generic achievement: namely, the extent to which autobiography, more than any other form of narrative, takes up the problem of depth— not by raising depth to an absolute present where it would become mere surface, but by enacting the reciprocity between depth and surface in what constitutes a cultural act of reading the self rather than a private act of writing the self. The reading of oneself is always a cultural reading since self-knowledge, far from

[2]Louis A. Renza, "The Veto of the Imagination: A Theory of Autobiography," *New Literary History* 9 (Autumn 1977), 1-26.

[3]See, for example, Jeffrey Mehlman, *A Structural Study of Autobiography: Proust, Leiris, Sartre, Lévi-Strauss* (Ithaca: Cornell University Press, 1974).

[4]Marjorie Grene, *The Knower and the Known* (Berkeley: University of California Press, 1974), p. 157.

being transcendent or free-floating, is always grounded in the signs of one's existence that are received from others, as well as from the works of culture by which one is him- or herself interpreted. Such views as I have mentioned—the one that assumes autobiography to be a private act of the self writing, the other that assumes autobiography to be part of a reified textual system—overlook the cultural dimension of the autobiographical act. They take into account neither the reading self of the autobiographer nor the reader we necessarily become when we set out to understand the autobiographical text. Henry David Thoreau became such a reader, a "faithful reader," as he named the activity. He became not only a faithful reader of Nature but, as I want to show, a faithful reader of the self.

I

Autobiography is a mode of fictional and historical narrative that delves into time in order to take up the problematic of depth. Ever since Augustine's *Confessions,* time has been recognized as both the medium and the subject matter of autobiography. The ordinariness of time is suggested in Thoreau's homely claim that "time is the stream I go afishing in." Not so ordinary, however, is his surprising suggestion that the bait he would use is the self. He is not fishing in time, then, for the purpose of catching the self and rescuing it from time's flux, as so many critics would define as a central goal of autobiography. The self is rather the bait Thoreau would use to catch something else in the medium of time. And what he would catch is Walden Pond, the "earth's eye" that represents for Thoreau reality itself. This eye is a mode of perception *into* which he would look for the purpose of measuring the "depth of his own nature," not an eye out of which he could achieve a worldless perspective.

With himself as bait, then, Thoreau will go afishing in time. He "hooks" himself for this expedition into autobiography in the opening page of his account when he adopts the first-person standpoint of speaking: "We commonly do not remember that it is, after all, always the first person that is speaking." With this reminder that would otherwise seem to be redundant in the context of *auto*-biography, Thoreau is calling attention, first of all, to the fact that speaking is the beginning of autobiography. Not only is language the matter of autobiography, but the self as language (the flesh made word, if you will) is its *form* as well. Or, to state the case in the negative, the language of autobiography is not to be understood as a third-person account of a life that just so happens to be one's own and that can be presented as though it were an objective entity, complete in itself, and existing in a perspectiveless world of other objects. Nor can the autobiographical act be construed as an effort to provide an accounting *after* the fact, as though the telling were simply a report on what has already taken place.

To view autobiography as simply a report on past events is to overlook the fact that autobiography takes place in the present. Thoreau's present-participial formulation, the first person *speaking,* represents the *nunc stans* of taking up one's situation in time. One does not thereby fix or close down one's life in the present moment as though speaking arises *de nouveau,* thus serving to arrest time in some static category. To understand autobiography as an act of speaking is to underscore its full temporality. Speaking takes place in time, constituting itself in the present, but deriving from the past and projecting itself into the future. As a single movement which incorporates that past into the present and "welds" that present to a future, speaking reenacts "the temporal style of the world."[5]

It is by means of language that life, as it were, is always in the process of catching up with itself. Catching up, however, is a matter not only of catching *back* to the past whose horizon makes room for the present, but of catching *forward* as well to the horizon of the future where " 'reality' always stands" as "observed and feared or, at any rate, [as] still undecided possibilities."[6]

The autobiographical act of bringing life to language involves a temporal gathering of what Hannah Arendt calls "the absent tenses," the "no-more" of the past and the "not-yet" of the future, into the fullness of the present.[7] The autobiographical present, however, is not to be understood as a fully explicited spatial habitat which is above or immune to the flux of time. To speak one's life is, rather, to take up occupancy within the mobile setting of time as depth.

[5]See M. Merleau-Ponty, *Phenomenology of Perception,* trans. Colin Smith (London: Routledge & Kegan Paul, 1962), pp. 421-24.

[6]Ibid., p. 101.

[7]Hannah Arendt, *The Life of the Mind: Thinking* (Vol. I), (New York: Harcourt Brace Jovanovich, 1978), p. 211.

II

Were one to look at autobiography as an act of space, language, it could be said, takes up that space and fills it, but not like filling a vessel that would otherwise be empty. The ever-present background of speech means that space is never simply empty or neutral. It is occupied and directed and therefore more accurately to be understood as *place*. In this respect, *Walden* is as much an autobiographical expedition into space as into time. Spatial imagery, in fact, abounds in Thoreau's work along with those boundaries that are presumed, often mistakenly, to define or more often to confine that space. When Thoreau records his desire to speak "somewhere without bounds," he is working not toward some boundless eternity of transcendental standpoint. One cannot, after all, wedge one's feet into everywhere. He is looking, rather, for that *one place* from which he will have access to everywhere. Or, as he puts it, he is searching for that "one fact" which if "you stand right fronting...face to face..., you will see the sun glimmer on both its surfaces...and feel its sweet edge dividing you through the heart and marrow, and so you will happily conclude your mortal career."[8] That one fact he discovers in the coming of spring and, in particular, in the thawing of the sand bank at the side of the railroad track. It is here, in this "one actual phenomenon," that he experiences the true nature of depth in all its fullness—a fullness which comes to expression as the *"dehiscence of time"* and which transforms space into sacred place.[9]

In the *Journal* entry of September 5, 1851, shortly before he undertook his major revision of *Walden*, Thoreau records his dream of achieving "a return to the primitive analogical and derivative sources of words."[10] Such an achievement was a goal held in common by the Transcendentalist circle which regularly gathered in Elizabeth Palmer Peabody's Boston bookstore during the 1830s and '40s. The influence of German Idealism and Swedenborgian correspondences was evident in their attempts to formulate a philosophy of "natural

---

[8]Henry David Thoreau, *Walden and Civil Disobedience,* ed. Sherman Paul (Boston: Houghton Mifflin Co., Riverside Editions, 1960), p. 67. Subsequent citations will be indicated by page numbers directly following the quotations in my text.

[9]The phrase comes from Merleau-Ponty, *Phenomenology of Perception,* p. 421.

[10]Bradford Torrey and Francis H. Allen, eds., *The Journal of Henry D. Thoreau* (14 vol., bound as 2), (New York: Dover Publications, Inc., 1962), p. 462.

language" which would contravene the Lockean understanding of words as arbitrary signs invented for social communication. Most persuasive for the Transcendentalists' understanding of language was Herder's thesis, in *The Spirit of Hebrew Poetry,* which Miss Peabody had translated, that the roots of language are to be found in nature itself. This thesis finds expression in Thoreau's famous passage on style in his essay, "Walking":

> Where is the literature which gives expression to Nature? He would be a poet who could impress the winds and streams into his service, to speak for him; who nailed words to their primitive senses, as farmers drive down stakes in the spring, which the frost has heaved; who derived his words as often he used them—transplanting them to his page with earth adhering to their roots....[11]

These lines on the poet's activity recall much of Thoreau's conduct in the first sixteen chapters of *Walden:* As expressed in the "Walking" passage, the forceful nailing and driving fulfills the requirement Thoreau makes of himself as well as his readers when he admonishes them to live life *deliberately.* Not only must he and his readers bring conscious purpose to their unthinking lives; such purpose must be carried out with the near-military vigor he brings to that familiar statement of purpose: "I went to the woods because I wished to live deliberately, to front only the essential facts of life;...to live so sturdily and Spartan-like as to put to rout all that was not life" (62-63). The Spartan warrior in this early *Walden* passage is the same commander who, in the "Walking" essay, would "impress the winds and streams into his service."

But there is yet another part of this passage on natural style, this time having to do with the effect of the words on the "faithful reader" rather than with the treatment they would have at the hands of the poet. In the second half of the passage, Thoreau writes that these "words were so true and fresh and natural that they would appear to expand like the buds at the approach of spring, though they lay half smothered between two musty leaves in a library,—ay, to bloom and bear fruit there, after their kind, annually, for the faithful reader, in sympathy with surrounding Nature."[12]

In contrast to the downward thrust of nailing and driving that is

---

[11]Jeffrey L. Duncan, ed., *Thoreau: The Major Essays* (New York: E.P. Dutton & Co., Inc., 1972), p. 214.
[12]Ibid.

intended to anchor the poet's words in the substratum of Nature—a thrust that suggests a calculated decisiveness and not a little violence —the words appear to the "faithful reader" in quite another way: as emerging and expanding in a process that, far from being abrupt and the result of deliberate planning, is slow and spontaneous.

Here, then, we have a completion of the twofold activity that characterizes the *Walden* experiment. As I shall demonstrate in the remainder of this essay, Thoreau's autobiographical experiment in *Walden* has to do with his becoming this "faithful reader." He meets that goal in his "reading" of spring, an experience which constitutes for him an event of language that discloses the "temporal style of the world." This "style" is the mediator of depth; the coming of spring constitutes that "one fact" which reveals "the infinite extent of our relations."

There are many passages in *Walden* where Thoreau makes quite clear his interest in language: "It would seem," he writes in a late chapter, "as if the very language of our parlors would lose all its nerve and degenerate into *parlaver* wholly, our lives pass at such remoteness from its symbols..." (p. 167). Much earlier, he has already put the question, "Who knows but if men constructed their dwellings with their own hands, and provided food for themselves and families simply and honestly enough, the poetic faculty would be universally developed, as birds universally sing when they are so engaged" (p. 31). Midway between these two passages, in "The Beanfield," he remarks, "...some must work in fields if only for the sake of tropes and expression, to serve a parable-maker one day" (p. 112). What is striking in all three instances is the way Thoreau grounds his interest in language, whether it be the "language of our parlors" or the "poetic faculty," in the ordinariness of daily experience, particularly house building. Further highlighted in the correspondence between language and house building (and cultivating beans) in the notion of foundation which is the very source of this inner-outer process. And it is here that the relation between language and depth becomes more clear, a relation that is reciprocal. Not only does language come out of depth, but language ("I want to make the earth speak beans") is what puts one back in touch with depth as well. On his beans, Thoreau writes, "They attached me to the earth, and so I got strength like Antaeus" (p. 107).

Language, then, derives its power, Antaeuslike, from its rootedness in the earth. And conversely, one gains access to this rootedness by way of language, out of those forms of expression (house building, bean growing, poetry making) that make manifest, bring to the surface the under-the-soil source of all true expression. There are countless examples of the foundational metaphor throughout *Walden*. The central project of the book might, in fact, he described as the efforts—almost always deliberate, as I have already noted—to reach those foundations, to "live deep," as Thoreau puts it. These efforts can be seen in the early lyrical passage on wedging one's feet downward:

> Let us settle ourselves, and work and wedge our feet downward through the mud and slush of opinion, and prejudice, and tradition, and delusion, and appearance, that alluvian which covers the globe, through Paris and London, through New York and Boston and Concord, through church and state, through poetry and philosophy and religion till we come to a hard bottom and rocks in place, which we can call reality, and say, This is, and no mistake. ... Be it life or death, we crave only reality. (p. 67)

And in more detailed and literal description, Thoreau's "ontological scavenger-hunt" can be noted in the soundings of the bottom of Walden Pond.[13] "It is remarkable," he had observed, "how long men will believe in the bottomlessness of a pond without taking the trouble to sound it" (p. 195). Having himself taken such trouble in the dead of winter and by means of a hole cut in the ice, Thoreau seems to have edged closer to that "one fact," to the "This is, and no mistake" that he had earlier announced as the goal of his wedging. His final testimony in "Conclusion," that "there is a solid bottom everywhere," would seem to complete his experiment and make it possible for Thoreau to leave Walden for other lives.

But the sounding he was able to take—the Pond, he recorded, was "exactly one hundred and two feet deep"—is *not* the "one fact" that could bring to an end his "mortal career." As Thoreau himself is quick to note of this "remarkable depth for so small an area," it is still the case that "[w]hile men believe in the infinite some ponds will be thought to be bottomless" (p. 196). Notwithstanding the Cartesian-like probing of this "wedging" passage, the *"point d'appui"* that he would achieve depends not so much on *what* he sees as the *way*

---

[13]Walter Benn Michaels, *"Walden's* False Bottoms," in *Glyph* I, eds. Samuel Weber and Henry Sussmen (Baltimore: The Johns Hopkins University Press, Johns Hopkins Textual Studies, 1977), p. 136.

he sees it. He is interested, he says, in "carv[ing] and paint[ing] the very atmosphere and medium through which we look. ..." Or as he puts it in his Journal entry of September 13, 1852, "What I need is not to look at all, but a true sauntering of the eye."[14] Taken alone, this entry is misleading and actually contradicts the "habit of attention" to which Thoreau refers in an earlier part of this entry, a habit he has "to such excess that my senses get no rest, but suffer from a constant strain." The strain of attention is evident throughout his *Walden* account. The moralist who complains that [o]ur life is frittered away by detail" is at the same time the naturalist who painstakingly records in minutest detail the behavior of hooting owls, the size and density of animal skins, and the freezing dates of Walden Pond.

As for the itinerancy implied by the "true sauntering of the eye," Thoreau recorded elsewhere his belief that "to appreciate a single phenomenon, you must camp down beside it as for life. ..."[15] Such a camping down we find, for instance, at Thoreau's woodpile site from which he observes, much like Swift's Gulliver in the minaturized world of the Lilliputians, the "internecine war" between the armies of ants, "the red republicans on the one hand, the black imperialists on the other."

Applied biographically to what he does at Walden, then, the statement which contrasts looking with the sauntering eye makes little sense. But as a statement regarding his interest in language as the "very atmosphere and medium through which we look," it is central to his autobiographical goal. That goal is "to lay the foundation of a true expression." The coming of spring and, in particular, Thoreau's observations on the thawing of the sand bank at the edge of the railroad track, discloses such a foundation.

In that same 1852 *Journal* entry he writes, "Go not to the object, let it come to you." To be sure, Thoreau must sustain that state of "morning wakefulness" and "infinite expectation" which qualify him for the "highest art," namely, "to affect the quality of the day." At the same time, he must break the "habit of attention" that tends to domesticate "the vastness and strangeness of Nature." Nothing short of total disorientation will accomplish this break and make possible the "wise passivity" that contrasts so strikingly with the militarylike

[14]Torrey and Allen, *The Journal of Henry D. Thoreau*, p. 350.
[15]Quoted by Quentin Anderson, "Practical and Visionary Americans," *The American Scholar* 45 (August 1976), 409.

deliberations which superintend his activities leading up to spring. "Not till we are lost," he writes—and the New Testament allusion is unmistakable—"in other words, not till we have lost the world, do we begin to find ourselves, and realize where we are and the infinite extent of our relations" (p. 118). Having tried to make a home *in* Nature by going in so many ways to the object, Thoreau's autobiography will finally be a home *for* Nature when he lets the object come to him.

Dramatizing Nature "in full blast" and representing the fullest portrayal of the relation between language and depth, the passages on the thawing of the sand bank bring together all the major themes and movements of the book: the temporal unfolding of the hours, days, and seasons, and the spatial unlayering of geography, history, geology, and myth. At the conclusion of his observations he is able finally to announce, "[t]here is nothing inorganic." And having experienced "this one hillside" that "illustrated the principle of all the operations of Nature," Thoreau can report:

> The earth is not a mere fragment of dead history, stratum upon stratum like the leaves of a book, to be studied by geologists and antiquaries chiefly, but living poetry like the leaves of the trees, which precede flowers and fruit,—not a fossil earth, but a living earth.... (p. 210).

Spring's arrival announces itself first from a distance, in the "startling whoop" of ice breaking on the Pond, a sound as "loud as artillery" that Thoreau hears in the night. He had been attuned for this sound from the beginning of his sojourn: "One attraction in coming to the woods to live was that I should have the leisure and opportunity to see the Spring come in" (p. 206). All of his arrangements, one can now see in retrospect, have been geared to this event: the building of a house to conserve that "vital heat" which will find its correspondence in Nature's "great furnace," the cultivation of morning wakefulness when "there is a dawn in me" that will enable so close an observation of Nature as to "anticipate" her, the meditation on getting lost in the woods so as to "begin to find ourselves, and realize where we are and the infinite extent of our relations." Preparatory as well have been Thoreau's deliberate efforts to find the solid bottom —his "wedging" his feet "downward" and his cutting through the frozen ice to sound the Pond, along with his careful excavating and recording of the layers of historical and mythical events (from the building of the railroad to the prelapsarian creation of Walden Pond) that have preceded his own coming to the Pond and have served to hold him in place. All of this, "the perpetual instilling and drenching of the reality that surrounds us," has served to ready him for spring. And what he finally comes to experience more than confirms his credo, announced much earlier in "What I Lived For," that "[t]he universe constantly and obediently answers to our conceptions; whether we travel fast or slow, the track is laid for us. ..." (p. 67).

But what is finally most significant about his experience of spring is the extent to which its "extra-vagance" outstrips his conceptions, leading him at the end of his account to conclude that "[t]he universe is wider than our views of it" (p. 218). For unlike his earlier *deliberations,* by which he sought intentionally to peel away the layers that conceal the depth of Nature, the thawing of the sand bank reveals Nature's *own* intentions. The dramatic movement of spring is upward and outward—"The very globe continually transcends and translates itself, and becomes winged in its orbit"—a counter to the winter inwardness and the downwardness of Thoreau's wedging and sounding.

What the *manifest*ation of Nature in spring has to suggest, *contra* Bergson, is not simply that the surfacing of depth by way of language is *not* the losing of depth but, on the contrary, that it is the bringing of depth to fullest expression. But what is more, spring testifies to what is at the heart of depth's concealment, namely, that *depth exists in anticipation of becoming surface,* lying in wait to burst forth in the manifest language of leaves: "No wonder that the earth expresses itself outwardly in leaves, it *so labors* with the idea inwardly" (p. 209, italics mine).

What Thoreau comes to realize constitutes the very center of the autobiographical project, operating both as its source and its *telos.* He has finally come to experience in the dehiscence of depth what has been all along the "already there," that anchorage in temporality which enables him to engage in such a project in the first place. What initially pre-tended itself as necessarily concealed below the surface, a surface through which his early strategies—both physical and linguistic—were designed to penetrate, finally presents itself *as* surface, there all the while but awaiting that *gaze* which could see it, a seeing made possible by the "atmosphere and medium" of the language of Nature that Thoreau has made his own.

Thoreau had earlier observed of the surface of Walden Pond that "not a pickerel or shiner picks an insect from this smooth surface but it manifestly disturbs the equilibrium of the whole lake. ... Not a fish can leap or an insect fall on the pond but it is thus reported in circling dimples, the lines of beauty, as it were the constant welling up of its fountain, the gentle pulsing of its life, the heaving of its breast" (pp. 129, 130). The tautness of *Walden's* narrative surface, compressing as it does the actual experience of several years into one and harkening back to Thoreau's earliest memories at the age of four, itself records such minute undulations.[16] And like the lake which is the "landscape's most beautiful and expressive feature," Thoreau's autobiographical narrative is the "earth's eye, looking into which the beholder measures the depth [of all things, including] ...his own nature" (p. 128).

If Nature is the foundation of "true expression," there is finally no going behind language to its origins. Nature—or reality—makes itself known only through its own language, its speaking "beans" or its expression in leaves. The foundation that Thoreau himself can lay is constituted by the interpretive act of his own autobiography —an act of reading more than an act of writing. In words that are "derived" as often as they are "used," he can become that "faithful reader, in [such] sympathy with surrounding Nature" that his own life can be synecdochal for the lives of others, not in providing the exact pattern to which those others must fit their own, but in urging other acts of reading. Only in the risk of interpretation—"what we have to stand on tip-toe to read and devote our most alert and wakeful hours to" (p. 72)—will men and women be rescued from their "quiet desperation" and assured "[t]here is more day to dawn."

III

In a 1956 essay which marks a watershed in modern theory of autobiography, Georges Gusdorf defines what he calls the "condit-

---

[16]For the idea of the narrative structure itself as a kind of surface, I am indebted to Professor Wesley Kort of Duke University. Thoreau writes of his childhood memory of the Pond: "It is one of the oldest scenes stamped on my memory" (p. 107). I might add that the writing history of *Walden*, as well as the expanse of life history, which is compressed in the account, contributes to the density of its textural pressure. As J. Lyndon Shanley and others have pointed out, Walden represents the condensation of seven or eight years of revisions. Its materials go back to *Journal* entries that date from April 1839, a good six years before Thoreau took up residence by the pond.

ions and limits" of the genre.[17] With respect to the *conditions* for understanding autobiography, Gusdorf argues that the literary features of the genre must be placed in the larger context of its anthropological dimensions. As for the *limits* of autobiography, Gusdorf uses the myth of Narcissus to portray the risks of self-reflection. Narcissus drowned, after all, in his overreach for the watery image he fell in love with.

Thoreau provides his own version of the Narcissus myth in the anecdote which helps to conclude his autobiographical excursion. His is a story about a traveller, a boy, and a swamp:

> We read that the traveller asked the boy if the swamp before him had a hard bottom. The boy replied that it had. But presently the traveller's horse sank in up to the girths, and he observed to the boy, "I thought you said that this bog had a hard bottom." "So it has," answered the latter, "but you have not got half way to it yet." (p. 225)

Thoreau goes on to make clear the allegorical intent of the anecdote. "So it is," he suggests, "with the bogs and quicksands of society; but he is an old boy that knows it." The allegory extends as well to the "bogs and quicksands" of interpretive activity—not only to the risks of autobiographical self-reading, but to the risks of reading any text. In either case, one is confronted with the problems of locating and gaining access to past meaning.

Is the truth of the past to be located, then, in an originating situation that lies somewhere behind the facade or, in the terms of the anecdote, below the surface of the present? Such would seem to be the case in that understanding of autobiography which assumes the self to be a private and, finally, transcendent modality—a modality which, like certain conceptions of genre, is unaffected by (because unaffiliated with) culture.[18] For both the Bergsonian theorists of autobiography and the categorist critics of genre, there is, indeed, a hard bottom. While the former deny any possibility of getting to

---

See Shanley, *The Making of Walden* (Chicago: University of Chicago Press, 1957) and Mutlu Konuk Blasing, *The Art of Life: Studies in American Autobiographical Literature* (Austin: University of Texas Press, 1977).

[17]The English translation of Gusdorf's essay is now available in James Olney, ed., *Autobiography: Essays Theoretical and Critical* (Princeton: Princeton University Press, 1980), pp. 28-48.

[18]I have in mind such conceptions of genre as those of Northrop Frye and E.D. Hirsch, who practice a "hermeneutics of the innocent eye." See Frank Lentricchia, "The Historicity of Frye's *Anatomy,*" *Salmagundi* 40 (Winter 1978), 97-121.

that bottom *alive,* the latter are sanguine about reaching the generic foundation of meaning so long as the diver divests him or herself of day-to-day attire and dons the proper dress.[19] Moreover, this meaning supposedly remains stable, whatever the cultural flotsam and jetsam floating above it. Indeed, it is possible and necessary to wedge oneself through these cultural accretions in order to gain access to the truth of the past.

Although it was this wedging strategy that impelled Thoreau's experiment at the outset, it is also his autobiographical excursion that calls it into question. The *"point d'appui"* he wanted initially to secure turns out to have its liabilites. In reaching the bottom "with rocks in place," the autobiographer, like Narcissus, runs the risk of drowning in certainty. Moreover, this Archimedean strategy gives the lie to that "momentum of temporality" which characterizes all interpretive activity and, in fact, makes it possible at all. Neither the past nor the present simply stays put.

Throughout *Walden,* Thoreau employs the image of the traveller to portray the writer's career. The image applies to the reader as well—both to the autobiographer as reader of his or her life and to the critic who provides yet another reading of the autobiographical text. As Frank Kermode has recently put the matter, "we interpret always as transients."[20] While traveling has its pleasures of discovery and rediscovery, it has its risks as well, particularly the risk of false or premature destination, as the swamp story suggests. In light of this kind of warning, the constraints against our ever reaching the bottom are reassuring as well as limiting. "No one," Kermode writes, "however special his point of vantage, can get past all those doorkeepers [of hermeneutical constraints imposed by culture, convention, ideology, and so on] into the shrine of the single sense. . . ."[21] The opacity that always characterizes one's relation to the past, to texts, and, indeed, to the world we live in is precisely what grounds one in the task of interpretation. That "lurking opacity behind what can be clearly formulated" enjoins us to have it out with the world in the sense-making activity that marks us as human and cultural

[19]The "proper dress" would be that of the "interpreter" whom E.D. Hirsch, for instance, distinguishes from the "biographical" person who simply reads. See *Validity in Interpretation* (New Haven: Yale University Press, 1967), p. 243.

[20]Frank Kermode, *The Genesis of Secrecy: On the Interpretation of Narrative* (Cambridge: Harvard University Press, 1980), p. 145.

[21]Ibid., p. 123.

beings. The possibility of loss no less than the prospects for recovery make of autobiography—or of any act of interpretation—the *vital* activity that it is.

One interprets because one is committed to understanding. Rising to occasions rather than getting to the bottom more accurately accounts for the motive of interpretation. Rising to occasions, of course, involves its own set of risks, as the myth of Antaeus—perhaps the more appropriate paradigm for autobiography—tells us. Antaeus was a giant who remained invincible as long as his feet remained on the earth. Many tried to defeat him, but even when he was knocked down, he would rise again with renewed strength. Knowing the secret of his strength, Hercules was able to defeat him by raising him up in the air. When Thoreau "stands on tip-toe to read" his own life, he stands Antaeuslike in the depth of full temporality—not on "truth remote," but at the "now and here" where "all...times and places and occasions" are to be found.

American Autobiography and Ideology

by Thomas P. Doherty

Autobiography is not a peculiarly American literary form, but it does seem to be a form peculiarly suited to the traditional American self-image: individualistic and optimistic. The individualism intrinsic to the genre finds a ready and sympathetic hearing in a society that—at least in its own popular imagination—aggrandizes the individual as the foundation of political and economic life. American autobiographies tend to be warmly reassuring: the very fact of an autobiography testifies both to the value of the individual and to possibilities for success in the culture (failures do not get published). In a democratic culture the implicit message is that *an* autobiography has worth not just as an exemplar, but in itself. Benjamin Franklin, probably the cagiest of American autobiographers, capitalizes on this sentiment at the same time that he is helping to solidify it: "As constant good fortune has accompanied me to even an advanced period of life, my posterity will perhaps be desirous of learning the means, which I employed, and which, thanks to Providence, so well succeeded with me," he announces by way of justification at the beginning of his *Autobiography*. "They may also deem them fit to be imitated..."[1] Franklin's audience shares his faith in the efficacy of individual action in a free society— a faith that is nowhere stated explicitly. Franklin's portrait of himself as an aggressive actor in a society of possibilities became a model "fit to be imitated" not only for his readership, but for other autobiographies in the American tradition as well. His "faith" is not in Providence—which any Connecticut Yankee will read as "luck" anyway—but in himself and his country. Franklin is sly

"American Autobiography and Ideology", *by Thomas P. Doherty* appears for the first time in this volume. It is used by permission of the author.

[1]Benjamin Franklin, *Autobiography and Other Writings*, ed. Russell B. Nye (Boston: Houghton Mifflin Company, 1958), p. 1.

enough to render his fulsome self-confidence as a mild character flaw that only makes him the more human and likable. In the process he established a pattern for popular American autobiography, a pattern characterized by an implicit affirmation of the worth of the individual and of capitalistic success and the systems that allow for it.

Though every autobiography is in one sense or another "ideological," American autobiography is, by and large, surprisingly non-ideological when it comes to the specifics of political and economic critique. Those autobiographies that go against the American grain — against the assertion of self, the values of a success-oriented culture, and the attendant political structures — are few and far between. Certainly, ideological currents can be traced in American autobiographies from Franklin to Sammy Davis, Jr. — but even those autobiographies that are most disenchanted with the American way of life are oddly silent about the political and economic structures that help determine that way of life. This implicit acceptance of the political superstructure is at base conservative, tending to reenforce a particular political reality merely in reiterating its presentation. Henry Adams, though light-years away from Franklin's optimistic boosterism, expresses his dissatisfactions in ways that are primarily temperamental, individualistic — and, ultimately reactionary. In the American tradition, one must turn to the slave narratives of the first part of the nineteenth century to find an expression of a reaction to political realities that also suggests (and this is the crucial point) political *remedies*. Franklin and Adams both criticize society, and by extrapolation that critique might have real political consequence. But neither suggests what is to be done. Even the slave autobiographies propose political action in delicate terms. Frederick Douglass's autobiography concludes with his "sincerely and earnestly hoping that this little book may do something toward throwing light on the American slave system and hastening the glad day of deliverance."[2] (To be sure, William Lloyd Garrison is far more rebellious in his introduction — but his race and status mitigate his cry of "law or no law, constitution or no constitution."[3]) The American historical tradition may be rich in rebellion and revolutionary critique. The American autobiographical tradition is either outright conservative

---

[2] Frederick Douglass, *Narrative of the Life of Frederick Douglass* (New York: Anchor Books, 1973), p. 124.

[3] Ibid., p. xi.

or, if counter to the prevailing ideological winds, basically theoretical in its dissatisfaction. Only the outcasts and outlaws seem to arrive at a revolutionary critique of society that addresses problems and proposes solutions that redefine the political terms of American life. If the above can be accepted as hypothesis, the next stage of this investigation is explanatory: why does autobiography, at least in the American tradition, tend to be ideologically conservative? By way of contrast, two autobiographies that are avowedly radical may prove illuminating: Alexander Berkman's *Prison Memoirs of an Anarchist* and George Jackson's *Soledad Brother*. For all their differences, Berkman's and Jackson's autobiographies are alike in one fundamental way: their opposition to the political order is basic and manifests itself in political action. Unlike the abolitionists, Berkman and Jackson want change that will totally reorder society and not just affect one sphere of influence. This trait of articulated opposition to specific economic and political superstructures (capitalist democracy) defines revolutionary critique and separates this kind of autobiography from the more personal and philosophical opposition that Adams and Thoreau voice in their life stories.

In exploring the ideological patterns in these two autobiographies, two concepts from James Olney's study of the meaning of autobiography, *Metaphors of Self,* may prove useful. The first is a matter of methodology, the second a philosophical framework. Methodologically, Olney rejects formal analysis and any kind of historicism. This is not to say that textual problems are to be ignored, merely that for Olney the best way to view an autobiography is "to see it in relation to the vital impulse to order that has always caused man to create and that, in the end, determines both the nature and form of what he creates."[4] This "impulse to order" takes two characteristic forms as revealed in autobiography. There are those autobiographies of the "single metaphor" (autobiography simplex) and those of the "double metaphor" (autobiography duplex). The essential difference between the two types centers on Olney's concept of the *daimon,* which he defines as the autobiographer's "personal genius and guardian spirit, a dominant faculty or function or tendency that form[s] a part of [the] whole self and from which there [is] no escape."[5] This is the daimon of the simplex autobiographer. For the

---

[4]James Olney, *Metaphors of Self* (New Jersey: Princeton University Press, 1972), p. 3.

[5]Ibid., p. 39.

autobiographer duplex, however, the daimon "can only be described as the self."[6] Olney's idea of the self is part Jung, part Jefferson, part Keats—and wholly amorphous. This "self" lives symbolically in the metaphorical structure of the autobiography and is "greater than the sum of all its various parts."[7] But perhaps any definition of the self is bound to be vague around the edges. For the purposes of this investigation, we can recognize the daimon of the simplex autobiographer as analogous to (sometimes identical with) what the more politically minded would call *ideology*. The duplex autobiographer has a daimon that is less easily articulated: the meaning of duplex autobiographies is apprehended not through the narrative story but through the complex interconnections of symbol and metaphor that (re-)create the autobiographer in the autobiography.

One would be doing Olney a disservice to separate his method from the philosophical framework in which it operates. His paradigm arises out of what the philosopher Heraclitus termed the *Logos,* which might be crudely rendered as "the ordering principle in life." To Olney, the Logos of the autobiographer is synonymous with the very meaning of an autobiography. As he expresses it:

> In every individual, to the degree that he is an individual, the whole principle and essence of the Logos is wholly present, so that in his integrity the whole harmony of the universe is entirely and, as it were, uniquely present or existent. What the Logos demands of the individual is that he should realize his logos—it is the Logos. If one takes...four notions together—the intimate relation of self-knowledge and cosmology; the flux of all the world; the "becomingness" of the self; the identity of logos and Logos—Heraclitus's conclusion is logical and wholly human, the conclusion of the philosopher and the artist, the conclusion, more simply, of the autobiographer and the man...[8]

In short, Olney's own *daimon* is the *Logos.* In appropriating Olney's *daimon* paradigm, we shall be forced to accept some of his philosophical framework. However, we shall not be concerned here so much with his philosophical superstructure—of which the daimon is but one element. Rather, the focus will be on the peculiar problems of an autobiography whose daimon is unmistakably

[6]Ibid., p. 39.
[7]Ibid., pp. 6-7.
[8]Ibid., pp. 6-7.

political in purpose. How the avowed ideology of Berkman's *Prison Memoirs of an Anarchist* (1912) and Jackson's *Soledad Brother* (1970) intersects with their respective autobiographical daimons will, it is hoped, illuminate the effect that the autobiographical act has on the ideologue and his ideology.

Alexander Berkman's *Prison Memoirs of an Anarchist* is a unique autobiography by any standards. It is an engrossing narrative that manages to combine a revolutionary critique of the American economic system with the most intense kind of personal (re)evaluation. More unusual, though, is the book's masterful artistry: it makes nearly any restatement of the work border on the reductive. Berkman's use of language to delineate character, his facile manipulation of symbol and metaphor, and his adroit handling of a variety of literary styles and techniques is of a caliber generally found only in the most finely wrought fiction. As literature alone it compares favorably with anything published at the turn of the century. As an autobiography of an ideologue, it is well-nigh unparalleled. This is no *pro forma* bow to esthetics: in considering the ideology of the book, Berkman's authorial control should never be underestimated. "Naive revelation" notwithstanding, *Prison Memoirs* is as carefully constructed a personal-political statement one is likely to come across.

Berkman's autobiography gives eloquent testimony to the fact that political ideology can be a complex and ever-evolving world view. Indeed, it is just this realization that the protagonist comes to during the course of his imprisonment. As the book opens, Berkman is at pains to re-create dramatically for the reader the precise condition of the ideological mind. As the young anarchist rides into Pittsburgh to assassinate Henry Clay Frick, Berkman jumps cinematically from the hot and stuffy train to the feverish interior monologue of his narrator:

...the very life of a true revolutionist has no other purpose, no significance whatever, save to sacrifice it on the altar of the Beloved People. And what could be higher in life than to be a true revolutionist? It is to be a *man*, a complete MAN. A being who has neither personal interests or desires above the necessities of the Cause; one who has emancipated himself from being merely human, and has risen above that, even to the height of conviction which excludes all doubt, all regret;

in short, one who in the very inmost of his soul feels himself revolutionist first, human afterwards.[9]

Even as he heads toward the *attentat,* that loneliest of political acts, the narrator goes to extraordinary lengths to deny his uniqueness as an individual. Berkman's autobiographical portrait of the ideological mind is a vivid rendering of a psychological state which Erik Erikson was to express formulaically a half century later:

> By "ideological," I mean here a highly charged attitude rooted essentially in a general need for a world view coherent enough to attract one's total commitment and to render forever unnecessary the upsetting swings in mood and opinion which once accompanied identity confusion. ... But our commitment gets in the way of our investigatory ethos whenever and wherever we begin to prescribe for others what they must observe so as to guarantee the right conclusions or what they must avoid observing lest they might conclude the unmentionable.[10]

Erikson's formulation can provide a key insight into the relation of autobiography to ideology. The ideological commitment, as Berkman knew from experience, mandates not just a coherent world view, but a suspension of investigatory inquiry (Erikson's "investigatory ethos"): "even to the height of conviction which excludes all doubt." But the autobiographer is engaged in an investigation of his own experience that must, if nothing else, reveal to him the uniqueness of his own experience—at *least* in the particulars of his life. An autobiographer who adheres to an ideology that discounts particulars and rejects the idea of individual importance is engaged in something of a contradictory enterprise.

Of course, Berkman's portrait of the young anarchist rushing towards his destiny in Pittsburgh is a distanced re-creation of a man he no longer is. If there were not this distance between author and narrator, *Prison Memoirs* might be little more than an expressive political tract; in Olney's terms, an "autobiography simplex," grounded in a single metaphor of revolutionary anarchism. Further, the *daimon* of the work would be downright schizophrenic, for the mandates of Berkman's anarchism run counter to the mandates of

---

[9]Alexander Berkman, *Prison Memoirs of an Anarchist* (New York: Shocken Books, 1970, pp. 7-8. Further citations in the text are from this edition.

[10]Erik H. Erikson, *Life History and the Historical Moment* (New York: W. W. Norton & Co., Inc., 1975), p. 258.

the autobiographical act. Berkman breaks out of the simplex pattern into the duplex pattern when his narrator recognizes the identity of *logos* and *Logos*—in Berkman's terms, the identity of *people* and *People*. As the years in prison wear on and the young anarchist matures, he is kept alive by a bitter resentment and, he comes to realize, a growing dependence on his comrades—"his affections." The ideologue in him actively fights this lest he "conclude the unmentionable." The narrator recalls a dispute with his "Twin," a comrade in ideology whose "bourgeois predilections" ("Twenty cents for a single meal!") have angered him. He prescribes for his friend what he must observe:

> The revolutionist has no personal right to anything. Everything he has or earns belongs to the Cause. Everything, even his affections. Indeed, these especially. He must not become too much attached to anything. He should guard against strong love or passion. The People should be his only great love, his supreme passion. Mere human sentiment is unworthy of the real revolutionist: he lives for humanity .... (p. 73)

Berkman completes his autobiographical depiction of the ideological mind by showing the degree to which his personality (Erikson's "investigatory ethos") is truncated: even his "Twin" must draw the right conclusions or face censure.

The young anarchist's fierce prescription to his Twin reveals the depth of his commitment and will later be juxtaposed with the unmentionable conclusions he eventually comes to. Berkman's genius as an autobiographer is his ability to re-create and make credible this change in world outlook. His present-tense narrative allows the reader to experience—and the autobiographer to reexperience—the mentality of the ideologue and the process by which he comes to recognize his logos. There is ironic distance certainly—the words he spoke to his Twin must have come back to haunt him—but when the young anarchist speaks these words they accord fully with his experience up to that point. Berkman must lead his autobiographical self through a whole series of encounters and psychological states before he can plausibly render the change that the narrator goes through. The anarchist will come to reject most of his own prescriptions, but this rejection is no sudden change of world outlook. It is a slow process of costly self-knowledge: there is no great epiphany. The acute reader can discover the beginnings of the narrator's realizations almost before the narrator himself articulates them: his letters to the Girl, his relations with his fellow prisoners, and the scope of his thinking trace a rising arc of self-realization. "Daily association dispels the myth of the 'species,' and reveals the individual," (p. 2) he notes at one point, almost unaware of the consequences the observation will have on his ideology. By the time the narrator expresses his change in outlook verbally, he is merely making explicit a realization he has long been acting out. When his partner in escape dies suddenly, the narrator is shattered—and confused that the news of Bresci's revolutionary execution of the King of Italy rouses little interest in him. Almost reluctantly he confesses to himself:

> ...I feel that the individual, in certain cases, is of more direct and immediate consequence than humanity. What is the latter but the aggregate of individual existences—and shall these, the best of them, forever be sacrificed for the metaphysical collectivity? (p. 399)

Berkman must make it clear, however, that the narrator has not switched one ideological state for another. In Olney's terms, the recognition of one's logos is a flowing, not a static process. In recognizing the identity of people and People, the autobiographer duplex must also recognize and come to terms with his own self. The narrator of *Prison Memoirs of an Anarchist* must undergo yet *other* self-doubts and confusions: it is, in a sense, a journey that never ends. The self is ever "becoming." The narrator's release from prison is not the transport he had anticipated: his inability to enjoy his freedom puzzles and finally sickens him. The changes in the movement and in himself bring him to the edge of self-destruction. On his sickbed, he listens to the Girl's review of the changes the last fourteen years have wrought in anarchism. "It is merely a change of form," she tells him, "the essence is the same. We are the same as before, Aleck, only made deeper and broader by years of experience" (p. 510). The essence of which Emma Goldman spoke—whether analogous to Olney's idea of the Logos or not—does provide the narrator with the emotional sustenance he needs to persevere in life and the movement. Though he has ideals, he is no longer "ideological." His commitment to anarchism is still strong, but it is not all-pervasive. There will be dedication, but no prescriptions. Fourteen years in prison have taught him—and the autobiographical act has reiterated—that the self is characterized by "becomingness." Though he will never again know the certainty of the ideological mind, the freedom from the identity confusion he experienced upon his release, he will likewise never again confuse the "metaphysical collectivity" with the "individual existences."

Berkman's autobiography illustrates the genre's tendency to weaken the force of a revolutionary critique made through the prism of personal experience. The narrator's politics evolve from simplistic anarchism to an insightful analysis of the specific nature of economic power in the United States. By the time of the McKinley assassination, the narrator is offering truly thoughtful and original observations about "the scheme of political subjection" in America. For the most part, though, these observations take on a secondary importance when weighed against the personal development of the narrator. In an autobiography, the overriding concern is with the autobiographical persona: the thought becomes background material for the self; the ideas in the work cannot displace attention from the developing ego. Both Hutchins Hapgood and Paul Goodman, in their respective introductions to *Prison Memoirs of an Anarchist,* treat the book more as a "human document" than a political one. Berkman the autobiographer is no longer the one-dimensional ideologue who attempted to kill Frick; but he is still, as the title indicates, very much a man who defines himself in terms of his political ethos. The political thinking of the author Berkman warrants serious consideration. In taking the book to be a plea for, say, prison reform, one is highly underestimating Berkman's still-fierce opposition to the American system. In following the magnificent story of what Goodman calls human "rubber and bounce," one can miss the power of the political conclusions about America that Berkman the autobiographer has come to. The autobiography ends with the narrator rededicating himself to his work; it is indicative of the nature of autobiography that the *kind* of choice he finally makes is less remembered than the fact that he has regained a sense of self and purpose. The relentless individualism of the genre subordinates all other considerations.

Prison Memoirs of an Anarchist is, finally, a work more about the ideologue than his ideology. Berkman is artist enough to appreciate the limitations of the autobiographical genre in rendering complex political ideas: he knows that any first-person narration will implicate the reader more in individual experience than in political theorizing. Also, as a true autobiographer duplex, his main concern (though not the *only* concern) *is* the ever-becoming self. In turning to another avowedly ideological autobiography—George Jackson's *Soledad Brother*—we shall observe an autobiographer actively fighting against this tendency of autobiography to aggrandize the ideologue at the expense of his ideology.

Soledad Brother is a very different sort of autobiography. The discontinuous epistolary format, the rigors of prison censorship, and Jackson's own motivations in writing *Soledad Brother* all mitigate against the kind of paradigm James Olney suggests as a way to apprehend the meaning of such enterprises. Unlike Berkman's work, Jackson's autobiography is an in-progress production: he isn't so much *re*-creating a self as creating one as he goes along. Moreover, Jackson is consciously working in opposition to the American autobiographical tradition in those sections of *Soledad Brother* that are explicitly autobiographical—the introductory section ("Recent Letters and an Autobiography") and, presumably, in the selection and ordering of materials. It is this attitude of Jackson's, more than censorship and the epistolary format, that makes *Soledad Brother* so problematic "as autobiography." In effect, he wants to create an autobiographical form that has no "self." The degree to which he fails to remove his "self" from *Soledad Brother* reaffirms the power of the genre to delineate personality, regardless of authorial intent.

"I don't recognize uniqueness," Jackson writes at the opening of his autobiography, "not as it's applied to individualism, because it is too tightly tied into decadent capitalist culture."[11] The statement signals *Soledad Brother's* central and explicit *raison d'être*: it is a highly charged ideological statement that is autobiographical on the surface only. Jackson is a Marxist of the historical materialist variety: deterministic, pseudoscientific, pledged to violent confrontation with the exploitative capitalist system, and—selfless. His autobiography will be no solipsistic exercise in self-expression, but a powerful political treatise designed to awaken and not to edify. "Investigation of anything outside the tenets of the fascist system itself is futile," he writes (p. 35)—and the subjects he writes about are all, to him, imcomprehensible without this primary knowledge. Racism is stamped inalterably into the American sociopolitical and

---

[11]George Jackson, *Soledad Brother* (New York: Bantam Books, Inc., 1972), p. 10 Further citations in the text are from this edition.

economic system; related problems of crime and poverty arise out of a dialectically predetermined set of economic circumstances.

Looking at Jackson's critique, one is struck by two simultaneous yet contradictory thoughts: first, as a political thinker, Jackson is something of an ideological parrot; second, despite the first qualification, his critique has a resonance and force out of all proportion to the power of the actual thinking. The force of Jackson's critique comes, paradoxically, from the very thing that he is trying to suppress: his individual voice. The Marxist ideologue has chosen a literary form, autobiography, that builds its structure not from the imperatives of Marxist historicism, but from the experience of the individual life. Like Berkman, he has also embraced an ideology that denies individual uniqueness. For a man of Jackson's announced beliefs, the autobiographical act itself borders on ideological heresy. As he asks himself: "How can I explain the runaway slave in terms that do not imply uniqueness?" (p. 10).

His answer is to submerge the self in ideology and to make the story of his personal life into a revolutionary model. By becoming an exemplar and idealizing himself, Jackson neatly circumvents the "uniqueness" question:

> I am [the] victim, born innocent, a *total* product of my surroundings. Everything that I am, I developed into because of circumstantial and situational pressures. I was born knowing nothing; necessity and environment formed me, and everyone like me. (p. 104)

As *Soledad Brother* progresses, Jackson becomes more and more conscious of his symbolic status as a victimized Everyman. In the last letter to his lawyer, he makes it explicit:

> Don't mistake this as a message from George to Fay, it's a message from the hunted running blacks to those people of this society who profess to want to change the conditions that destroy life. (p. 247)

In Erikson's terms, Jackson's allegiance to Marxism is a bulwark against "identity confusion"—a phrase that doesn't quite capture the quality of the vicious daily psychological and physical threats to Jackson's person. Given the extremity of Jackson's prison existence, his detachment from his "uniqueness" allows him one other advantage: survival. In perhaps the most illuminating passage in the entire work, the author writes:

...in the passing of these last couple of years, I have completely retrained myself and my thinking to the point now that I think and dream one thing only, twenty-four hours of each day. I have no habits, no ego, no name, no face. I feel no love, no tenderness for anyone who does not think as I do. There can be no ties of kinship strong enough to move me from my course. (p. 101)

Like the lecture Berkman the young anarchist gives to his "Twin," Jackson's prescription is a classic—and unconscious?—depiction of the ideological mind. The difference between the young ideologue of the opening section of *Prison Memoirs of an Anarchist* and the adult idealogue of *Soledad Brother* is that Berkman's ideological mind fits the Eriksonian formula; Jackson's ideology serves first and foremost as a survival adaptation. Indeed, as Sidonie Smith points out, "In society where blackness is met with implicit and explicit forms of racism, the understanding of that very racism, its motivations, its effects upon the self and the society at large, is tantamount to the understanding of one's identity."[12]

For Jackson, identity means *control:* the word sounds over and over again in his letters. Though Jackson has the capacity to see himself as a symbol, he is not blind to the fact that he himself is a real, not a symbolic victim. Jackson's ideology may dictate that he submerge his uniqueness (at least theoretically) in the "metaphysical collectivity," but throughout *Soledad Brother* there is a forceful countertendency that emerges despite Jackson's self-effacing pronouncements. In his early letters this tendency manifests itself almost exclusively through his revolutionary critique of white, capitalistic society; again, the critique is commonplace, but the force of Jackson's language makes it unique. Further, as a self-educated black prisoner in an overtly racist environment, he speaks with a moral force unique to his person and situation (imagine a white college student delivering the same critique). In his early letters, there is an ironic tension between Jackson the Marxist ideologue and Jackson the autobiographer expressing a self. In the letters to his mother especially, Jackson can flip-flop between bombastic "destroy the malefactor and root out his ideals" lectures to the tenderest kind of self-revelation:

[12]Sidonie Smith, *Where I'm Bound* (Westport, Conn.: Greenwood Press, 1974), p. 120.

> I do not think of myself as one small person among so many. I know what I can do, I know I can build and can cause things to happen, but I also can be hurt. (p. 86)

His letters to his father seldom voice such moments of self-doubt and revelation, but they are no less full of the self:

> Control over the circumstances of my existence is of the first importance to me. Without this control, or with control in someone else's hands, I am forever insecure, subject at times to the whims of the man in control, and you and I know how whimsical some men can be. (p. 101)

Jackson may confess to insecurity, but the fundamental thrust of passages like these—and his letters are full of them—is a rebellious assertion of the individual self: Jackson's. Most important, it is through this creation of an autobiographical self that Jackson manages to attain some measure of the control lacking in his daily prison existence. Jackson's daimon is precisely this: the impulse to control. His autobiographical letters allow him to impose an order on his life impossible in reality.

Soledad Brother is, by its very structure, an autobiography simplex. Jackson's need for control—expressed both in his ideological world view and in his creation of an autobiographical self—determines the course of the work. Towards the end of the book, as Jackson's correspondence and literary sophistication broaden, he makes a beginning toward what James Olney calls the recognition of the identity of Logos and logos (or what Berkman called the identity of people and People). But Jackson is not in the same position as the young anarchist: the attacks on him are unrelenting, and purely as a survival adaptation he cannot yet reject the ideology that supports him in prison. Having chosen a literary form that intrinsically aggrandizes the self, Jackson's last letters are often self-contradictory: part critique and part counter to the theory of that critique. He remains the fierce ideologue—suggesting that Angela Davis portray Martin Luther King as a Maoist, telling Joan to doctor his past letters—and, simultaneously, he becomes more open in expressing the affection and understanding he has for his correspondents. In the end, one is left with the feeling of nothing so much as thwarted possibilities.

Regardless of the ideology, the idealogue who is truly interested in criticizing society and gaining adherents would do well to choose a genre other than autobiography. Those autobiographies that are the *least* overtly ideological, paradoxically, seem to have the most forceful and longest-lasting influence. Franklin's implicit acceptance of the political order is a far more telling point that Berkman's explicit rejection of the same. Especially if the ideology subordinates the individual to the Cause, autobiography is, almost by definition, a self-defeating enterprise. The power of narrative and the reader's natural identification with the autobiographer will nearly always make one care more about the ideologue than the ideology.

To Be Black and Blue:
The Blues Genre
in Black American Autobiography

by Elizabeth Schultz

The history of Afro-American autobiography is long and full. A recent bibliography of black American autobiographies, for example, lists 417 works written between 1865 and 1973, and the Fall 1974 publication of Angela Davis's *Autobiography* and Nate Shaw's life-story in *All God's Dangers* indicates that black Americans continue to feel that the autobiography is an efficacious means for conveying their views of their relationship with society.[1]

In America in the eighteenth and nineteenth centuries, thousands of former slaves set down the history of their escape from bondage into freedom in writings which came to be called "slave narratives" and to be identified as an independent literary genre; the first of these was printed in 1705, and the last was Booker T. Washington's memorable *Up from Slavery* (1901).[2] In the 1930s,

"To be Black and Blue: The Blues Genre in Black American Autobiography" by Elizabeth Schultz, from *Kansas Quarterly*, 7, no. 3 (Summer 1975), 81-96. Reprinted by permission of *Kansas Quarterly* and the author.

[1]See Russell G. Brignano, *Black Americans in Autobiography: An Annotated Bibliography of Autobiographies and Autobiographical Books Written Since the Civil War* (Durham, N.C.: Duke University Press, 1974); Angela Davis, *Angela Davis—An Autobiography* (New York: Random House, 1974); and Theodore Rosengarten, ed., *All God's Dangers: The Life of Nate Shaw* (New York: Alfred Knopf, 1974).

[2]See Arna Bontemps, "The Slave Narrative: An American Genre" in *Great Slave Narratives* (Boston: Beacon Press, 1969), pp. vii-xix; Gilbert Osofsky, "Puttin' On Ole Massa: The Significance of Slave Narratives," in *Puttin' On Ole Massa* (New York: Harper & Row, 1969), pp. 9-48; and "Southern Views of the 'Peculiar Institu-tion': A Study in Black and White," the introduction for *Five Slave Narratives* (New York: Arno Press, 1968), pp. i-xxiv, for general discussion and analyses of the written slave narratives.

however, the genre was further expanded by the addition of over 2,000 oral narratives: the interviews with former slaves which were conducted as part of the Federal Writers' Project of the Works Progress Administration and collected in over 10,000 pages in the Library of Congress.[3] The written and the oral autobiographical narratives may be considered antecedents for two differing modes within the rich genre of black autobiography, with Davis's *Autobiography* and Shaw's reflections of his eighty-six years being the modern-day descendants of the two modes. The emotional drive of the written narrative, as with traditional church testimonial, is toward the reader or listener, whereas the impact of the oral narrative, as with traditional blues, is first upon the individual writer or singer himself; the former assumes an external community, whereas the latter seeks to create a community through the sharing of psychic experiences in the process of their articulation. Black autobiography, then, has a testimonial as well as a blues mode.

In both the written and the oral autobiographies, however, the individual discovers himself to be and describes himself as a member of the black community. Traditional autobiography, called "a distinctive product of Western post-Roman civilization,"[4] focuses emphatically upon the individual, although Stephen Spender notes that even the autobiographical confession is "from subject to object, from the individual to the community or creed."[5] Characteristic of the black autobiography, however, is the fact that the individual and the community are not polarities; there is a community of fundamental identification between "I" and "We" within any single

---

[3]See B. A. Botkin, *Lay My Burden Down: A Folk History of Slavery* (Chicago: University of Chicago Press, 1945) and Norman Yetman, "Introduction" to *Life Under the "Peculiar Institution": Selections from the Slave Narrative Collection* (New York: Holt, Rinehart, & Winston, 1970), pp. 1-6, for discussion and analyses of the interviews with ex-slaves in the WPA collection. Note that the collection is being published in 16 volumes under the editorship of George P. Rawick with the title *The American Slave: A Composite Autobiography* by the Greenwood Press in Westport, Connecticut.

[4]Roy Pascal, *Design and Truth in Autobiography* (Cambridge, Mass.; Harvard University Press, 1960), p. 180. In his general study of the genre of autobiography, Pascal neglects to recognize that the tradition of autobiographical writings has continued in Japan since the tenth century, and in discussing Western autobiography, he ignores the black American autobiography entirely.

[5]Stephen Spender, *The Making of a Poem* (London: Hamish Hamilton, 1955), p. 69.

autobiography in spite of differences in autobiographical modes and in the autobiographers' visions. St. Clair Drake maintains:

> The genre [of the Afro-American autobiography] is one in which more intimate aspects of the autobiographer's personal experience are subordinated to social commentary and reflections upon what it means to be a Negro in a world dominated by white men. There have been no black Marcel Prousts and André Gides. The traumatic effects of the black experience seem to have made confessional writing an intellectual luxury black writers cannot afford.[6]

In its development, all black autobiography might be compared to the development of the blues; LeRoi Jones, noting that traditional African songs deal "with the exploits of the social unit," points out that in America the African began to sing songs concerned with his own personal exploits:

> ...the insistence of the blues verse on the life of the individual and his individual trials and successes on the earth is a manifestation of the whole Western concept of man's life, and it is a development that could only be found in an American black man's music. ...The whole concept of the *solo*, of a man singing or playing by himself, was relatively unknown in West African music.[7]

Black autobiography in general, however, like the blues, expands the solo; the voice of the single individual retains the tone of the tribe. Of Richard Wright's autobiography, *Black Boy* (1945), Ralph Ellison says that it is, like the blues, "an autobiographical chronicle of personal catastrophe expressed lyrically," but that "in it thousands of Negroes will for the first time see their destiny in public print."[8]

---

[6]St. Clair Drake, "Introduction" to Claude McKay's *A Long Way from Home: An Autobiography* (New York: Harcourt, Brace, & World, 1970), p. x. William W. Nichols, in his essay "Individualism and Autobiographical Art: Frederick Douglass and Henry Thoreau," *CLA Journal*, 16 (1973), p. 158, regarding the black American autobiographer's concern for the community, comments, "It seems to me that Douglass is so deeply concerned with exploring the complexity and perversity of human relationships that he simply cannot entertain the idea of an insular self. Maybe another way of putting it is to say that Douglass never shares that part of the American Dream which emphasizes the sovereignty of the individual will."

[7]LeRoi Jones (Imamu Amiri Baraka), *Blues People* (New York: William Morrow & Co., 1963), p. 66.

[8]Ralph Ellison, *Shadow and Act* (New York: Signet Books, 1966), pp. 90 and 104.

The written slave narrative, however, and those autobiographies of the late nineteenth and twentieth centuries written in a similar mode seek explicitly to change the destiny of the community. As in a traditional church testimonial, the intention of the autobiographer's description of his experience of conversion and salvation in these works is to bring his audience to a like conversion and salvation; consequently the particular facts of personal experience are generalized through logic or exaggeration, so that listeners or readers may readily grasp their significance. The revelations of slave narratives and their autobiographical successors also have the tone of urgency typical of testimonials: Be Saved or Perish in Hell; Find Freedom or Die in Slavery. The apparent intention of the testimonial autobiography thus seems to be to make the experiences of a personal history felt with revolutionary impact upon the present and the future.

The general theme of the written slave narratives, as Arna Bontemps explains, is "the fetters of mankind and the yearning of all living things for freedom."[9] Their specific theme, however, is the abolition of slavery, and as a result, they were widely used in the nineteenth century in support of the Abolition Movement. Through eyewitness accounts or the accounts of firsthand experiences, through practical polemics or impassioned rhetoric, the autobiographers' conviction remains the same as that of former slave Gustavus Vassa who concluded his *Life* (1789) with the following very simple, very powerful words: "The abolition of slavery would be an universal good."[10] At the outset of his autobiography, the testimonial writer is fully conscious of his conclusion, with each subsequent description or argument being used as evidence to contribute to the final irrefutability of his initial premise; the writer, in reflecting on his slave past, can view that past only from the perspective of his own freedom and therefore directs every word he writes to obtaining freedom for his brothers and sisters. Thus the horrors of slavery overshadow even Vassa's early memories of his beautiful African homeland and his gracious tribal life; in the testimonial autobiography, the end is truly in the beginning, for the tone of urgency must be sustained through the work and beyond.

Testimonial autobiographies of the late nineteenth and twentieth

[9]Bontemps, p. xviii.
[10]Gustavus Vassa, *The Life of Olaudah Equiano, or Gustavus Vassa, the African,* in Bontemps's *Great Slave Narratives,* p. 190.

centuries have the same general theme as the written slave narratives, but their specific themes vary. Freedom, for example, in Washington's *Up from Slavery* is freedom to join the American middle class in things economic, whereas in Leslie Lacy's *Rise and Fall of a Proper Negro* (1970) it is freedom from hypocritical middle-class materialistic and aesthetic values; in W.E.B. Du Bois' *Autobiography* (1968), as in Angela Davis's *Autobiography*, it is freedom from capitalistic oppression; in Malcolm X's *Autobiography* (1964) it is freedom from the illusion of white supremacy and toward the development of a powerful black community, and in Donald Reeves's *Notes of a Processed Brother* (1971) it is specifically freedom from a white supremacist educational system. In the autobiographies of Marshall W. "Major" Taylor, Lt. William J. Powell, Matthew A. Henson, W.C. Handy, and Mary Church Terrell, whom Rebecca Chalmers Barton in the first full-length study of black autobiography, *Witnesses for Freedom,* calls "The Achievers," it is freedom to prove their individual worth.[11]

Often in these testimonial autobiographies, the personal voice is subsumed by the writer's desire to minimize himself because of the urgency of his theme. Not only are intimate facts of personal history omitted, but lengthy documents or newspaper accounts are included to prove objectively the historicity of a specific theme. Thus W. E. B. Du Bois curtails a discussion of his personality to a single chapter entitled "My Character," but presents such historically valuable resolutions as those concerning the founding of the Niagara Movement or those concerning a program of race studies at black colleges in the South.

As with Vassa's *Life*, the beginning of the testimonial autobiography anticipates the conclusion. Malcolm X, therefore, opens his *Autobiography* with an account of the Ku Klux Klan terrorism of his family's home at the time he was in his mother's womb and of his father's early dedication to Garveyism; it seems, therefore, that he was destined even before birth to become an effective spokesman for the Black Muslims and for black consciousness. Chronology may be purposefully shifted—an episode from the writer's maturity placed at the beginning of the autobiography—so that early events in a lifetime can be contemplated through the determining filter of that most significant later event. Leslie Lacy's autobiography thus

[11]Rebecca Chalmers Barton, *Witnesses for Freedom: Negro Americans in Autobiography* (New York: Harper & Brothers, 1948), p. 43.

opens with a description of his on-the-spot reaction to Nkrumah's downfall in Ghana, and Du Bois begins with a description of his eye-opening trip to the Soviet Union and the Republic of China, which is followed by an "Interlude" set in italics explaining his commitment to Communism, "a planned way of life in the production of wealth and work designed for building a state whose object is the highest welfare of its people and not merely the profit of a part."[12] As Lacy's life as a racially insecure boy must be viewed through the impact of his memory of African revolution, so Du Bois's ninety-one years as a racially proud democrat in an oppressive democracy must be viewed through the memory of his experiences in communistic states.

The oral slave narratives as well as the late nineteenth- and twentieth-century autobiographies written in a similar mode, however, like the blues, do not seek to change their listeners' destiny. Although they testify to the marvel of the black American's capacity to survive the inequities and brutalities of racism and to survive with wit, imagination, exuberance, and grace, although they express a multitude of personal convictions, they do not expound abstractly. Taken together, the oral slave narratives are a compendium of the factual details of the day-to-day activities of plantation life, of the South during the Civil War, and of Reconstruction; of folklore generated in the black community; of vignettes of acquaintances and of family genealogies; as such they are an invaluable source of information for students of American history, as Eugene Genovese's *Roll, Jordan, Roll* (1974) amply exemplifies. The individual voice also sings out loudly in these narratives. B. A. Botkin says of the oral slave narratives:

> In some cases, as in the narratives of Millie Evans and Cato— — —, the ex-slave subordinates personal history to social history and tells what is true for all or most slaves. In other cases, like that of Katie Rowe, the ex-slave tells what is true of the individual life. And by putting the two together, one gets what a true life-history should give—not only the "organic reality of the person" but also a sense of the "growth of a person in a cultural milieu."[13]

[12]W. E. B. Du Bois, *The Autobiography of W. E. B. Du Bois* (New York: International Publishers, 1968), p. 57.

[13]Botkin, p. 60.

The narrators do not, in general, seem to feel compelled to press their evaluations of their experiences upon others, although, as Allen V. Manning recognizes in his narrative, "...some folks been taught one way and some been taught another, and folks always think the way they been taught."[14] Joanna Draper may conclude her account with the statement, "I never will forgive that white man for not telling me I was free,"[15] or Sarah Gudger begin her account with an assertion of her "hard life. Just work and work and work,"[16] or Mary Reynolds express in her final conviction that "I don't 'lieve they ever gwine have slaves no more on this earth. I think God done took that burden offen his black children, and I'm aiming to praise Him for it to His face in the days of glory what ain't so far off."[17] Nevertheless, the impetus of their stories is neither to incite rebellion nor to legitimize slavery nor to document God's Providence in the working out of human affairs; the intention of most of the narratives seems to be to give the "Genesis to Rev'lations, and it de truth, as I' members it",[18] to"...tell you all I can, but I won't tell you nothing but the truth";[19] to resolve their narrations with an explicit "Dat am de end of de road,"[20] a matter-of-fact "Here we is," or a recognition of a full life: "I'se eatin' white bread now and havin' de best time of my life. But wen de Lord say, 'Delia, well done; come up higher,' I'll be glad to go."[21]

If the testimonial autobiography is concerned with the objectification and development of a specific conviction, the blues autobiography is concerned with the process of discovering meaning, a process synonymous with the discovery of consciousness, with the reader implicitly being engaged in this process. James Olney explains that an autobiography "intentionally or not [is] a monument of the self at the summary moment of composition."[22] Ellison, in his essay on

---

[14]*Ibid.*, p. 98.
[15]*Ibid.*, p. 103.
[16]Yetman, p. 150.
[17]Botkin, p. 125.
[18]Yetman, p. 198.
[19]Botkin, p. 60.
[20]Yetman, p. 126.
[21]*Ibid.*, p. 135.
[22]James Olney, *Metaphors of Self: The Meaning of Autobiography* (Princeton, N.J.: Princeton University Press, 1972), p. 35.

Wright's autobiography, associates it with the blues, for like the blues, it "is an impulse to keep the painful details and episodes of a brutal experience alive in one's aching consciousness, to finger its jagged grain, and to transcend it, not by the consolation of philosophy but by squeezing from it a near-tragic, near-comic lyricism."[23]

The experiences related in the blues as in the blues autobiography are not unmitigatedly brutal; they are too staggeringly complex. The consciousness of the blues autobiographer, however, while not always aching, is always active and alert, always evolving. The blues singer or autobiographer, by articulating his experiences—by fingering them in his consciousness, by grasping to give them verbal or musical expression—makes them comprehensible to himself and to those who listen to him, and thereby he transcends them. In this sense they express what Ellison has said of both the blues and of Wright's autobiography, they reveal at once "the agony of life and the possibility of conquering it through sheer toughness of spirit."[24]

For the testimonial autobiographer, the experiences of the past must affect the future; for the blues autobiographer, the experiences of the past are part of a continuing present. It is comprehensible, therefore, that Frederick Douglass wrote his life-history four times and Du Bois wrote his three times, each time conclusively; yet they repeatedly revised as a new episode in their lives clarified their specific convictions and the means of resolving them. The blues autobiographer, on the other hand, seems to leave his life history open-ended, resolving it only by a continued willingness to embrace reality. Anne Moody, for example, typically concludes her *Coming of Age in Mississippi* (1968) with a verse from "We Shall Overcome" and her own questioning refrain, "I WONDER, I really WONDER."[25] Also, typically, the blues autobiographer may write his life-story in supplements. Thus the second volume of Maya Angelou's autobiography, *Gather Together in My Name* (1974), picks up at the conclusion of her first volume, *I Know Why the Caged Bird Sings* (1969) and the birth of her son; and the second volume of Langston Hughes's autobiography, *I Wonder as I Wander* (1956), is a continuation of his first volume, *The Big Sea* (1940), which ends with his statement of anticipation, "I let down

[23]Ellison, p. 90.
[24]*Ibid.*, p. 104.
[25]Anne Moody, *Coming of Age in Mississippi* (New York: Dell, 1969), p. 384.

my nets and pulled. I'm still pulling."[26] Likewise, Chester Himes's *The Quality of Hurt* (1972) is emphatically conceived of as a first volume and concludes *in medias res* with the searching question, "Where would I find that was safe?"[27] Charles Mingus's *Beneath the Underdog* (1971), which snares the reader into the flow of his consciousness by being written primarily in the present tense, is reputedly only a portion of an extensive manuscript which is ever in process; with his concluding words—" 'Later, Mingus.' 'Later, Girl...' "[28]—the ritualistic farewell between himself and Fats Navarro, who we know from an earlier reference is to die from tuberculosis and heroin—Mingus as well as the reader is forced to acknowledge life's relentless dynamics without tears.

The testimonial autobiographer may pause in a chronological reporting of the facts in his life-story to document them with outside accounts, as do Washington, Douglass, Du Bois, Malcolm X, and Reeves, or to include an essay or interview published independently, as do Gwendolyn Brooks in her *Report from Part One* (1972), Nikki Giovanni in her *Gemini* (1971), and Eldridge Cleaver in *Soul on Ice* (1968); the blues autobiographer, however, interrupts the chronological flow only to gather together personal opinions on such topics as "Love," "Religion," "My People! My People!," as do Zora Neale Hurston in *Dust Tracks on a Road* (1942), Taylor Gordon in *Born to Be* (1929), and Claude McKay in *A Long Way from Home* (1937). With the blues autobiographer, it seems that the very process of writing is the catalyst for formulating such topical chapters rather than any attempt at documentation or historical objectivity. The process of writing thus becomes a process for self-discovery.

In general, however, for the blues autobiographer, reality is so multidimensional, it cannot be categorized under abstract headings. In a number of blues autobiographies, such as Claude Brown's *Manchild in the Promised Land* (1965), Moody's *Coming of Age*, Horace Cayton's *Long Old Road* (1965), or Himes's *Quality of Hurt,* the autobiographers are so entirely caught up in the rush of re-creating the circumstantial events of their lives and their response to those events at the time of their occurrence that they seldom

---

[26]Langston Hughes, *The Big Sea* (New York: Hill and Wang, 1963), p. 335.

[27]Chester Himes, *The Quality of Hurt,* I (Garden City, N.J.: Doubleday & Co., 1972), p. 351.

[28]Charles Mingus, *Beneath the Underdog* (New York: Alfred Knopf, 1971), p. 366.

pause to reflect on their abstract meaning. The reader, gradually becoming conscious of an emerging personality, however, feels drawn into a complex human relationship. Not beginning with an *a priori* set of astrological, psychological, or political conclusions about themselves, the writers at times even seem surprised at the character which is revealed or at the implications of the circumstances. Thus Claude Brown realizes only in conclusion that fear had dominated his life of violence on the Harlem streets, and Anne Moody that resignation must not dominate hers, and Chester Himes that his "feelings are too intense. I hate too bitterly, I love too exaltingly, I pity too extravagantly, I hurt too painfully. We American blacks call that 'soul,' I thought deprecatingly."[29]

Other blues autobiographers depend, from the beginning of their works, upon a particular aspect of their character to act as a lens through which the confusion of experience can be perceived and the integrity of personality achieved. Charles Mingus, for example, opens his autobiography by explaining to a psychiatrist the divisions of his psyche; he describes his experiences subsequently from the perspective of a coolly objective "I" contemplating "Baby," "my boy," "my man," or "Charles." Mingus, consequently, seems actively trying to order the pulsating chaos of emotions and events in his life. In Maya Angelou's *Caged Bird,* time seems her alter-ego; her young self, amazed at the spectacle of life and confused by it, is viewed from the self-conscious perspective of an older self who comprehends or consoles with the fine irony of maturity. From such a perspective—from "the perch of time"—the trauma of childhood rape and the guilt ensuing from the subsequent betrayal of the rapist, her doubt about her own sexuality and her subsequent pregnancy become bearable episodes in the story of a girl's growing-up.

Henry James called his autobiography "the history of [an] imagination"[30]; so might Richard Wright have called *Black Boy.* Beginning a long list of purely natural sensory experiences early in the autobiography, Wright notes that "Each...spoke with a cryptic tongue."[31] Two more such lists follow, the last one a list of superstitions involving natural phenomena. Wright seems, in making

[29]Himes, p. 351.

[30]Henry James, *A Small Boy and Others* (New York: Charles Scribner's Sons, 1913), p. 112.

[31]Richard Wright, *Black Boy* (New York: Harper & Row, 1966), p. 14.

such lists as a boy, to be seeking for the organizing principle in the phenomenal world which would give him the means for understanding and controlling it. His interpretations are inevitably emotional—in terms of his delight, nostalgia, melancholy, disdain, alarm, glory, panic. As he grows, he begins to ask endless questions of the adults about him, needing more desperately to understand the social world. When his mother suffered a paralytic stroke, the event became "a symbol in [his] mind, gathering to itself all the poverty, the ignorance, the helplessness; the painful, baffling, hunger-ridden days and hours; the restless moving, the futile seeking, the uncertainty, the fear, the dread; the meaningless pain and the endless suffering" *(Black Boy,* p. 112). Slowly, therefore, by exercising his intuition and imagination, he discovers the means of understanding; the very act of interpreting, of private symbolizing, of searching for meaning gives meaning. Increasingly he realizes that his imagination propels his search for extended meaning. The first story he is told is "the first experience in my life that had elicited from me a total emotional response" *(Black Boy,* p. 48); his own fantasies become "a moral bulwark that enabled me to feel I was keeping my emotional integrity whole, a support that enabled my personality to limp through days lived under the threat of violence" *(Black Boy,* p. 84); finally it is the books of others which give him the courage to "feel things deeply enough to try to order my life by my feelings" when nothing in the "external world of whites and blacks, which was the only world that I had ever known,...had ...evoked in me any belief in myself" *(Black Boy,* p. 282). Like Brown, Moody, and Himes, like Mingus and Angelou, Wright has achieved at the end of his autobiography not a sense of his destiny, but a sense of his potentialities as the reader has achieved a sense of human potentialities.

The process of discovering meaning in the blues autobiography thus becomes closely associated with the process of discovering personal consciousness. Of the blues and Wright's autobiography, Ellison says "they fall short of tragedy only in that they provide no solution, offer no scapegoat but the self."[32] Writing on seven autobiographies, all of which satisfy the criteria of the blues autobiography, Barton argues that "the basic fact of [the writers'] individualism" has repressed their concern with racial considerations:

[32]Ellison, p. 104.

...[they] do not [preach] but live fearlessly according to their personal creeds. ...Not one of them fails to give the impression that he or she clings to a citadel of self, inviolable to misfortune and defeat. Within these boundaries, each is a monarch and rules according to whim. ...Instead of holding long discourses on the special hardships which the depression brought to the Negro people, they turn to the cultivation of their private interests.[33]

However, Ellison and Barton limit the perspective of the blues autobiographers. Their vision is not turned completely on themselves as is that of Augustine or Rousseau, Gide or Proust, or other redoubtable autobiographers of the Western tradition. Central to their self-cognition is their recognition of themselves in relation to racially conscious American society; discovery of their own identity is coincident with their discovery of the distinct fact of their people's identity. They neither flagellate themselves, as Ellison's statement seems to imply, nor extol themselves, as Barton's statement suggests; nor are they simply proving their existence through self-assertion, as does Michel Leiris, or by seeking release from isolation, as does Rousseau.[34] If, to use the key word from Ellison's autobiographical novel, *Invisible Man* (1952), they make themselves less invisible by discovering their consciousness in the process of writing their autobiographies, they also make the black community less invisible. Our ideas about both the black community and the white community are sharpened by reading a testimonial autobiography; but by reading a blues autobiography, our sense of the complex life of the black community and of human possibilities is deepened as the writer's life is so thoroughly permeated by his people's heritage.

Whether the autobiographer discusses his experiences in the human community around the world as do Langston Hughes, Claude McKay, James Weldon Johnson, and Chester Himes, or restricts himself to corners of the United States as do Anne Moody, Claude Brown, Richard Wright, or Maya Angelou, it is their experi-

---

[33]Barton, p. 164. The autobiographies are those of Elizabeth Laura Adams *(Dark Symphony)*, William Stanley Braithwaite *('The House under Arcturus')*, Taylor Gordon *(Born to Be)*, Juanita Harrison *(My Great Wide Beautiful World)*, Claude McKay *(A Long Way from Home)*, Era Bell Thompson *(American Daughter)*, and Zora Neale Hurston *(Dust Tracks on a Road)*.

[34]Susan Sontag argues that this is the thrust of Leiris's *Manhood*, developing her argument in her essay on that work in *Against Interpretation* (New York: Noonday Press, 1961), pp. 61-68; Spender's discussion of Rousseau appears in his essay on "Confessions and Autobiography" in *The Making of a Poem*, pp. 63-72.

ence in the black American community which shapes their vision. Zora Neale Hurston may seem to be tidying up her relationship with the black community by relegating her thoughts to a single chapter entitled "My People! My People!"; yet the first statement she makes about herself is, "I was born in a Negro town,"[35] and the first statement she makes about her upbringing indicates that racial considerations underscored her upbringing:

> Mama exhorted her children at every opportunity to "jump at de sun." We might not land on the sun, but at least we would get off the ground. Papa did not feel so hopeful. Let well enough alone. It did not do for Negroes to have too much spirit. He was always threatening to break mine or kill me in the attempt. My mother was always standing between us. She conceded that I was impudent and given to talking back, but she didn't want to "squinch my spirit" too much for fear that I would turn out to be a mealy-mouthed rag doll by the time I got grown. *(Dust Tracks,* pp. 28-29).

Hurston obviously reacted against her father's pragmatic view of race and imbibed her mother's lyrical optimism, expressed in the metaphors of their people's language. The "tales of God, the Devil, animals and natural elements" which she heard in the community churches and on the front porch of the general store, besides introducing her to the dynamics of black society, aroused her imagination as a child and led to her extensive research later into black folklore. It led to the throbbing evocation in her autobiography of the spirit of "Polk County. After dark, the jooks. Songs are born out of feelings with an old beat-up piano, or a guitar for a mid-wife. Love made and unmade. Who put out dat lie, it was supposed to last forever? Love is when it is. No more here? Plenty more down the road" *(Dust Tracks,* p. 189). Claiming in her conclusion no bitterness and no anger toward white society, she relies, however, upon the words of a Negro deacon in a folktale to explain her goals: " 'Oh, no Gabriel! dat ain't no way for you to do. I can do my own running, but you got to 'low me the same chance as the rest' " *(Dust Tracks,* p. 292).

The last chapter of McKay's *A Long Way from Home,* "On Belonging to a Minority Group," is not simply a compilation of impressions regarding the black American, as is Hurston's chapter; it is a culmination of his persistent disgust with the Western white

[35]Zora Neale Hurston, *Dust Tracks on a Road* (New York: Arno Press, 1969), p. 11.

world for psychologically repressing black peoples by categorizing them and of his persistent distress over the black Americans' failure to develop "a group soul."[36] Yet neither his disgust nor his distress can be considered the theme of his autobiography, for his theme, as he states it in his concluding paragraph, is more inclusive: "All my life I have been a troubadour wanderer, nourishing myself mainly on the poetry of existence" *(Long Way,* p. 354). Yet his racial consciousness has been the specific source of his wanderlust, for in Europe he had come to realize that his "main psychological problem ...was the problem of color. Color-consciousness was the fundamental of my restlessness" *(Long Way,* p. 245). And as he explains in his first chapter, this very wanderlust was the source of his art: "The spirit of the vagabond, the daemon of some poets, had got hold of me" *(Long Way,* p. 4). Being a "motherless child, a long way from home," as other black singers had been, became the means for the song, for the autobiography itself.

For Maya Angelou, the black community is the essential community. Her grandmother's "Store," where the community congregates before and after work for food and for gossip, is the center of her universe until she is thirteen, "people" come to the store: "People were those who lived on my side of town. I didn't like them all, or, in fact, any of them very much, but they were people. These others, the strange pale creatures that lived in their alien unlife, weren't considered folks. They were whitefolks."[37] Thus, a "lifelong paranoia was born in [the] cold, molasses-slow minutes" *Caged Bird,* p. 29) of watching a group of "powhites" try to shame her grandmother, but confrontation with a bigoted Arkansas dentist and with the discriminatory practices of the San Francisco cable-car company do not daunt her. At sixteen, she feels herself initiated into "the brotherhood of man" by living with a group of other homeless children—black, white, chicano—in a junkyard, but her appreciation of and wonder at her own people, which began with her love for her grandmother, does not stop growing. Her generalized descriptions of a church revival and a summer picnic convey the vigor of the entire black community. In a chapter midway in her autobiography, her momentarily mixed feelings of despair and shame on her graduation day at the seemingly hopeless future for

[36]McKay, p. 349.
[37]Maya Angelou, *I Know Why the Caged Bird Sings* (New York: Random House, 1969), p. 25.

young blacks in racist America are surmounted by her pride in her people when the Negro national anthem is sung; as she consciously joins her people in singing, she unconsciously, from her perspective, in time, also predicts her own future as a poet for her people:

> We survived. ...I was no longer simply a member of the proud graduating class of 1940; I was a proud member of the wonderful, beautiful Negro race. Oh, Black known and unknown poets, how often have your auctioned pains sustained us? Who will compute the lonely nights made less lonely by your songs or the empty pots made less tragic by your tales? ...It may be enough, however, to have it said that we survive in exact relationship to the dedication of our poets (include preachers, musicians, and blues singers). *(Caged Bird,* pp. 179-80)

The first confrontation with whites is, for several blues autobiographers, an emotionally jarring experience as well as the experience which catapults them into an awareness of particular ethnic groups as well as the possibility of a single human group. Taylor Gordon, out of Montana for the first time in his late teens, is refused service in a diner in St. Paul. His immediate reaction is one of anger, followed by a loneliness he can't describe: "I never felt like it since. It seemed as though everyone whom I knew had died at once."[38] Almost directly, however, he determines to find out "all the inside stuff on this thing," but he concludes finally that "my people were as hard to figure out as perpetual motion" *(Born to Be,* p. 173), and though he claims to be untroubled by "the Race Question" in the last pages of his autobiography, we sense that he continues to have many questions which his mere protestations cannot rationalize away. For Horace Cayton, however, from his first attempt "to enter the fairy land of whites"[39] by trying to shoot off firecrackers as a child with a white girl, there is no possibility of rationalization, for his sense of alienation from whites and his consequent sense of alienation from blacks pervades the over-fifty-year time span of his autobiography. Like Gordon, Cayton, too, was brought up in the relatively prejudice-free atmosphere of the West Coast, but his alternating feelings of mistrust of both blacks and whites keep him from affiliation with the predominantly white unions; with the Chicago black community, even though he had written extensively about it in *Black Metropolis* (1945); or with the United Nations,

[38]Taylor Gordon, *Born To Be* (New York: Covici-Friede Publishers, 1929), p. 68.
[39]Horace Cayton, *Long Old Road* (New York: Trident Press, 1965), p. 17.

where he came to believe that American blacks could be aligned with other Third World peoples. His anguished inner conflict continues to his conclusion in which he states to the white woman he loves and leaves: "Until Negroes have total equality, I'll be with them. What I'd like best, at this stage, would be to live as an individual—just a plain American without a special cause. But that's impossible, I guess." *(Long Old Road,* p. 399) For Charles Mingus, who also grew up in the West, being categorized as "nigger" one day on his way home from school brought him to the terrifying realization that others had the power to determine his identity. To restore the power to himself, he takes up a mirror and sees the mixed racial strains in himself as well as the fact that

> he was a little of everything, wholly nothing, of no race, country, flag or friend. ...All he wanted was to be accepted somewhere and he still wasn't, so fuck it! He became something else. He fell in love with himself. "Fuck all you pathetic prejudiced cocksuckers," he thought. "I dig minds, inside and out. No race, no color, no sex. Don't show me no kind of skin 'cause I can see right through to the hate in your little undeveloped souls." *(Underdog,* p. 66).

With his own identity intact, he can transcend the inequities of racism he meets in the musical world and resist the temptation of drugs his fellow musicians succumb to. His buoyancy results finally in a series of transcendent visions in the autobiography's conclusion —a paean of praise for music, "my soul's will to live beyond my sperm's grave" *(Underdog,* p. 343); a practical, down-to-earth plan of the perfect life outlined for his future wife; and finally a dialogue with Fats Navarro on the regenerative possibilities of life, in which it becomes apparent that he envisions community with the flux of all matter.

For Richard Wright, an awareness of white oppression seems to begin in his subconscious when he is a child; his early fears and guilt become embodied in a dream-image of "huge wobbly white bags, like the full udders of cows, suspended from the ceiling above me" *(Black Boy,* p. 13). Of his adolescence, he says,

> Nothing challenged the totality of my personality so much as this pressure of hate and threat that stemmed from the invisible whites. ...Tension would set in at the mere mention of whites and a vast complex of emotions, involving the whole of my personality, would be aroused. It was as though I was continuously reacting to the threat of

some natural force whose hostile behavior could not be predicted. I had never in my life been abused by whites, but I had already become as conditioned to their existence as though I had been the victim of a thousand lynchings. *(Black Boy,* pp. 83-84)

Yet Wright triumphs in his struggle to keep the forces of fear and anxiety from stripping him of his imagination or reducing him to the status of the white man's "nigger":

> The white South said that it knew "niggers," and I was what the white South called a "nigger." Well, the white South had never known me— never known what I thought, what I felt. ...No word that I had ever heard fall from the lips of southern white men had ever made me really doubt the worth of my own humanity. *(Black Boy,* p. 283)

As he flees the South, he imagines a wider community of mankind, one in which all peoples "might win some redeeming meaning for ...having struggled and suffered here beneath the stars" *(Black Boy,* p. 285).

Other blues autobiographers submerge their personal identities in a black communal identity. J. Saunders Redding opens his *No Day of Triumph* (1942) with a section describing his own life through his graduation from college and follows it with three sections describing his travels into the South where he visits black people in a variety of circumstances. Redding's journey is one undertaken for "spiritual wholeness" out of his sense that black intellectuals, in particular, "were spiritually homeless, dying and alone, each on his separate hammock of memory and experience."[40] His brief personal statement explicitly tells of his growing up, "hating and fearing whites" and "hating and fearing and being ashamed of Negroes," of losing all ability to comprehend human values because of the omnipresence of racism; the following 200 pages implicitly show his discovery of these values in the lives of the people he meets on his travels. The surroundings and the voices of these people become his own, their history his, their courage and timidity, joy and despair his; the record of the events in his own life ceases, except as his objective descriptions of his people and his dialogues with them must be understood as synonymous with his own life. The four sections of the autobiography have titles taken from black music— "Troubled in Mind," "Don't Be Weary, Traveler," "Poor Wayfarin'

---

[40]J. Saunders Redding, *No Day of Triumph* (New York: Harper & Brothers, 1942), p. 43.

Stranger," and "There Is a Balm"—suggesting not only a movement from confusion to resignation to despair to consolation in his personal life, but also his complete identification with the black community. Cleaver's *Soul on Ice*, which might be classified as a testimonial autobiography for the specificity of its theme and its extensive political analyses which are devoid of a personal voice, nevertheless has the overtones of the blues. His first chapter, "On Becoming," is an excruciating analysis of the effect of the racist myths about the black man and the white woman upon his own psyche; in the course of his work, Cleaver comes to generalize, to see that his own sickness is shared by other black men and indeed by the nation at large. He works through his own problem in the three profoundly moving love letters he writes to his lawyer, a white woman, and then, following the letters, in a series of essays, he attempts to work through the difficult problem for others. The first essay is an allegorical discussion among black men of the racist and sexual myths of American culture; following it is an objective analysis of these myths; a sociopolitical essay on the "convalescence" of the nation through the union of "white Mind and black Body"; and finally a sermon of praise and adoration "To All Black Women, from All Black Men," in which his singular voice is metaphorically raised into a chorus of black male voices.

The style of the blues autobiography, unlike that of the testimonial autobiography, also seems a blending of the single voice with the group voice. In the blues autobiography, as in the oral slave narratives, the individual's idiosyncrasies of speech merge with the cadences and idioms of black American speech. As blues singers Mississippi Fred McDowell or Mississippi John Hurt, Lonnie Johnson or Robert Johnson have distinctive singing styles and yet retain the inflections and rhythms recognizably belonging only to black American song, so are blues autobiographies both individualistic and ethnic in their style. By contrast the style of the testimonial autobiography is often that of the well-written editorial, its tone controlled by a reliance upon abstract generalizations and logic; the testimonial, written in the clear objective style of good journalism, would seem, therefore, easily translatable. Whereas the whole of Iceberg Slim's *Pimp: The Story of My Life* (1969) and Taylor Gordon's autobiography are written in dialect, demanding a glossary at the conclusion, Malcolm X, who spent years in Harlem as a hustler, gives only an isolated example of the hustler's cant along with his translation to illuminate a particular point in his argument, rendering the whole of his autobiography in the clear tones of impersonal history. The style of the blues autobiography may require special translation, and yet, ironically, like the oral slave narratives, the effect of their reliance upon language as it is spoken is to create a sense of dialogue and hence a sense of community with the reader.

Zora Neale Hurston's prose, for example, rings with the rhythms, the natural metaphors, and the anthropomorphisms of the black sermon, even as she exposes her very personal feelings to us. Of her mother's death and its effects upon her, she writes:

> Just then, Death finished his prowling through the house on his padded feet and entered the room. He bowed to Mama in his way, and she made her manners and left us to act out our ceremonies over unimportant things. ...But life picked me up from the foot of Mama's bed, grief, self-despisement and all, and set my feet in strange ways. *(Dust Tracks,* pp. 96-97)

In summing up her life, she says, fusing secular and sacred images: "I can look back and see sharp shadows, high lights, and smudgy inbetweens. I have been in Sorrow's kitchen and licked out all the pots. Then I have stood on the peaky mountain wrappen [*sic*] in rainbows, with a harp and a sword in my hands." *(Dust Tracks,* p. 288)

In Mingus's autobiography, the narrative sequences have the flow of uninterrupted speech, with his numerous re-created dialogues seemingly improvised against them; he seems therefore to be playing out a long jazz set in reverse, with the solo part doing the back-up work. His dependence upon the present tense, expletives, and the accretion of phrases and nouns also gives his prose the immediacy and vitality of a jazz composition. For example, in one short typical paragraph, his style involves the reader in the tension of a personal episode, an episode which the style also forces us to feel is typical of the history of black people in a racist society:

> Charlie Davis is playing a piano intro and just as Dan begins to sing Phil Moore's "Shoo Shoo Baby" Bo screams—"Oh God! That nigger's got a gun!" Shots ring through the room. The lighted juke box shatters. Glass spatters. People scramble under tables and rush toward exits. Before I know it my boy has calmly laid his bass down and is walking toward the gunman. "Man, you crazy?!" Bo shouts. "Get down! He shooting a gun!" The man is aiming right at him but looks

frightened and as Mingus yells "I'll kill you! I'll kill you! This is *Bo's* place!" he fires a wild shot and runs for the door. In the confusion outside a voice calls "Halt in the name of the law!" RAT TAT TAT! All is quiet. And another nigger lies dead in front of Bewley's Black Rooster. But as usual it's the wrong man, it's just poor Half-Pint, the bootlegger who supplies whiskey to the after-hour joints. *(Underdog,* pp. 195-96).

The understatement of "as usual it's the wrong man, it's just poor Half-Pint" is characteristic of the "near-tragic, near-comic lyricism," "the agony of life and...sheer toughness of spirit" which Ellison considers essential to the blues; such understatement is characteristic of the ironic tone underlying both the blues and the blues autobiography which gives the singer and the writer the means to endure. Thus Mingus can say of his own down-and-out condition in another instance with ironic self-deprecation: "Well, Popeye ate spinach and mayonnaise was mainly eggs. With economical eating habits like this [I] could survive" *(Underdog,* p. 181). Gordon can bear the horror on his first trip to the South only by indulging in self-mockery:

Every once in a while the porter in the Pullman car ahead of us would run back and tell me to look out of the window in different towns and see the amusing signs, like: "NIGGER—READ AND RUN," "NIGGER —DON'T LET THE SUN GO DOWN ON YOU HERE," "NIGGERS AND DOGS NOT ALLOWED." That last one made me feel very, very remorseful. I was a murderer of my kin. One day a dog ran in front of the car I was driving and he was killed. *(Born to Be,* p. 119)

Maya Angelou's quick sense of irony allows her to approach the memory of a particular humiliation on Easter Sunday with both anguish and laughter:

I tried to hold, to squeeze it back, to keep it from speeding, but when I reached the church porch I knew I'd have to let it go, or it would probably run right back to my head and my poor head would burst like a dropped watermelon. ...So I ran down into the yard and let it go. I ran, peeing and crying, not toward the toilet out back but to our house. I'd get a whipping for it, to be sure, and the nasty children would have something new to tease me about. I laughed anyway, partially for the sweet release; still, the greater joy came not only from being liberated from the silly church but from the knowledge that I wouldn't die from a busted head. *(Caged Bird,* pp. 5-6)

It also allows her to endure, with her people, the contradictions in their lives: "Go to church in that cloud of weariness? Not go home and lay those tortured bones in a feather bed? The idea came to me that my people may be a race of masochists and that not only was it our fate to live the poorest, roughest life but that we like it like that" *(Caged Bird,* p. 118). Or in another instance, following the victory of Joe Louis, she knows "It wouldn't do for a Black man and his family to be caught on a lonely country road on a night when Joe Louis had proved that we were the strongest people in the world" *(Caged Bird,* p. 132).

In the blues autobiography, the writers' expression of their sense of reality is intensely subjective; yet by the conscious exaggeration and selection of the details in the episodes of their lives, they create an objective correlative for the emotional ferocity of their experiences. Whereas the testimonial autobiographer strives to convey accuracy of historical fact, the blues autobiographer seems primarily concerned with the emotional accuracy of experience. Wright, recalling the story of a black woman's successful deception and destruction of four white men, legitimizes such writing by explaining, "I did not know if the story was factually true or not, but it was emotionally true because I had already grown to feel that there existed men against whom I was powerless, men who could violate my life at will" *(Black Boy,* p. 83). The autobiographies of Brown, Moody, and Iceberg Slim, with their clearly defined themes, might be said to border on being testimonials; yet their life-histories are, for the most part, devoid of abstract analyses and arguments. Their polemics can be considered only the polemics of experience.[41] With their themes argued only through the relentless accumulation of the concrete details of their lives, their lives become parables of experience rather than polemical theses about life. They seldom pause in their description of poverty and brutality, fear and shame to use such abstract words or to analyze the source of these physical and emotional conditions; yet their matter-of-fact descriptions of Harlem boys shooting drugs and each other, of girls in Mississippi spending long hours in domestic service, and of professional pimping activities in Chicago convey the intense desperation of such lives.

Angelou, attempting to recapture the intensity of her childhood

---

[41]Roger Rosenblatt's provocative title for a lecture delivered December 28, 1974, at the Modern Language Association meeting in New York was "Third World Autobiography: The Artifact and the Polemics of Experience."

feelings, seems consciously to seek the fantasy or the metaphor which will adequately suggest their emotional density. For describing her and her brother's trip into "white-folksville," she finds a childlike metaphor to suggest their fear of the unknown: "We were explorers walking without weapons into man-eating animals' territory" *(Caged Bird,* p. 24). Of her brother's significance to her life during her childhood, she writes with adult understanding of her needs, yet with childlike exaggeration: "Of all the needs (there are none imaginary) a lonely child has, the one that must be satisfied, if there is going to be hope and a hope of wholeness, is the unshaking need for an unshakable God. My pretty Black brother was my Kingdom Come" *(Caged Bird,* p. 23). Perhaps, however, the best example of the way in which her imagination ripens in keeping with the emotional necessity occurs when, taken by her grandmother to a white dentist who claims he'd "rather stick [his] hand in a dog's mouth than a nigger's," she visualizes in italics her grandmother's private confrontation with the dentist; in the conclusion of the fantasized version of this confrontation, her grandmother becomes a mythic heroine who cannot deign to kill the disgusting dragon of a dentist:

> *Momma pulled herself back from being ten feet tall with eight-foot arms and said, "You're welcome for nothing, you varlet; I wouldn't waste a killing on the likes of you." On her way out she waved her handkerchief at the nurse and turned her into a crocus sack of chicken feed. (Caged Bird,* p. 186)

In the autobiographies of Charley White *(No Quittin' Sense* [1969]) and Nate Shaw, both of which were written down from oral transcriptions, the genre of the oral slave narrative and the blues autobiography reaches fulfillment. The particularities of their lives are remarkably similar; both grow to manhood at the turn of the century in the rural South; out of love for their families and self-respect, both become highly skilled at various labors; and in the course of their long lives, both stand courageously against the inequities of racial oppression, believing not only in the necessity of justice but also in the possibility of change. Yet the integrity and vigor of White and Shaw as particular individuals emanates from their autobiographies. As each reflects back upon his personal history and relates the sequence of events comprising that history, a man stands forth, and the reader, in the process of absorbing their reflections, responds, at first, with the patience necessary in a grow-

ing and ripening friendship, and at last with awe at the realization
that the man he had taken for a friend is also a hero. White perhaps
comes most fully into being, with the essential goodness of his
character best revealed, when he speaks of his feeling at having
established "God's Storehouse" for the benefit of the community
poor:

> I got a tightening and loosening feeling along my arms and legs and
> up my back and over the top of my head. It was like the day I went to
> the baptizing on Bell Creek when I was three, and that time Mama
> was making my first pair of pants so I could go to school, and the night
> Gladys was born, and the other light and airy times all crowded up
> together.[42]

Shaw, who refuses so much more emphatically than does White to
be "disrecognized," to be made invisible by any societal force;
whose relationships with his family and with black and white people in his community, with animals and with the land, with the
dynamics of racism and capitalism are more complex, eventually
takes on human greatness. The resiliency of his character and his
essential goodness are exemplified in his clear-cut decision, at the
age of twenty-one, to leave the obligations of serving his somewhat
tyrannical father and become his own man:

> I was a poor young colored man but I had the strength of a man who
> comes to know himself, all in me from my toes to my head. I mean
> right and no wrong; I meant to get up and out [of] that old rut and act
> a man. I didn't want to marry no man and no woman's daughter, take
> her off and perish her to death because I couldn't support her, just an
> old hack through the world.[43]

His character—his sense of his and our humanity—however, continues to unfold through the autobiography. Proud, he also comes
to know the dangers of hubris when he finds himself in conflict
with the landed white interests because of his membership in the
Sharecroppers' Union: "I was climbin up in the world like a boy
climbin a tree. And I feel just as easy too" *(God's Dangers,* p. 285).
Yet he also knows that "[God] thought so much of you He gave you
knowledge He didn't give the other animals. And He gave you a

---

[42]Charley White and Ada Morehead Holland, *No Quittin' Sense* (Austin: Univer
sity of Texas Press, 1969), p. 167.
[43]Shaw, p. 83.

soul to save, He made you responsible to that knowledge: a man is responsible, a woman is responsible, for the acts of their flesh and blood and the thoughts on their minds." *(God's Dangers,* p. 228). He takes full responsibility for joining the Union and defending his land. In the conclusion of his autobiography,[44] he sees the meaning of his accumulated experiences with both pride and humility and shares this meaning with the reader: "But I have had my eyes open too long to the facts, and my ears, what I've heard; and what I have touched with my hands and what have touched me is a fact. And I treasures what I know and I so often think about it and how necessary it is to set an example before God and man." *(God's Dangers,* p. 554).

Nate Shaw's final revelation to himself and to us, his listeners and readers, is comparable to that in other blues autobiographies. The example he seeks to set—"before God and man"—must, to a great extent, be in his autobiography, for in the process of its creation he reveals himself fully, and in the process of our reading we discover him fully. As the facts of his life touched him, the emotional reality of his life also touches us, with the final triumph of the blues autobiography being that it not only confirms the individual's life and our common human life, but it also re-creates the link between the two.

[44]Nate Shaw's and Charley White's life-histories were transcribed and edited by others as, to a degree, the Abolitionists had assisted in writing some slave narratives and the WPA interviewers had influenced the responses made by former slaves. The reader of *All God's Dangers,* however, feels he can trust Theodore Rosengarten's sensitive editing and selecting of Shaw's memories in view of his concern to do "justice both to their occurrence in time and his sequence of recollection. I tried, within the limits of a general chronology, to preserve the affinities between stories" *(God's Dangers,* p. xxiv); the conclusion of his written narrative therefore would seem to be in keeping with Shaw's own sense of final culmination.

Inventing the Jew:
Notes on Jewish Autobiography

By Alvin H. Rosenfeld

The Jew does not invent himself. History invents the Jew. But who invents history? The Jew does. The Jew as the Lord of History? Yes. But surely that is a fiction! Precisely. And it is just this fiction, together with its counterweight of fact, that I want to explore in the pages that follow.

Before commencing, I must state that I do not use the term "fiction" in a way that is necessarily demeaning. Rather, I have in mind the sense of the term as understood by the American poet Wallace Stevens, who used it with reference to a conception of self and reality that is knowingly willed. Stevens refers to such acts of the will as "supreme fictions," products of noble imagination, and not mere wind-blown fancies. Such fictions, or imaginative inventions, are the work of poets, who have taken it upon themselves to construct verbal worlds of significance at a time when the world itself all too often seems to be devoid of coherence and sustaining purpose. In the face of an overarching meaninglessness, Art, in a word, comes to replace empty heaven and its hymns.

One further qualifying note must be registered before beginning: such fictions are allowed all the world's peoples except one—the Jews, who are not permitted to invent themselves. This is not to say that we do not try hard, or that we are unsuccessful at self-creation. We *do* try hard and are as skillful as anyone else, but we are not allowed to indulge ourselves ultimately in fabrication. Whenever we lose sight of that interdiction and overextend ourselves in imaginative play, history calls us back to our senses: thunderously. For that

"Inventing the Jew: Notes on Jewish Autobiography" by Alvin H. Rosenfeld, From *Midstream: A Monthly Jewish Review*, 21. no. 4 (April 1975) pp. 54-67. Reprinted by permission of *Midstream* and the author.

is the fate of the Jews, to vouch for the truths of history, truths that we help to establish *as* history, even if, as is often the case, we would prefer it otherwise.

For present purposes, I want to restrict the application of these thoughts to the art of autobiographical invention, more specifically, to modern Jewish autobiography. In America the pattern for such writing is established early in this century by two books, Mary Antin's *The Promised Land* and Abraham Cahan's *The Rise of David Levinsky*. Both are part of the broader literature of immigration, that heroic story of founding fathers that more often than not becomes an embarrassment and an encumbrance to native sons, who, in characteristic American fashion, seek whatever release they can gain for themselves from the precedence of European life, only to find that their new-won freedom usually dooms them to the vagaries and wastings of deracination and general spiritual impoverishment. The Jewish element in this story is a strong one, so much so that it has dominated American Jewish writing to date and alternately directed and impeded the major lines of its development.

Mary Antin's autobiography, a highly successful book that has gone through thirty-four printings and sold some 85,000 copies since its original publication in 1912, presents the idealist version of this story. Born Maryashe, called Mashke, the daughter of Hannah Hayye, in Polotzk, Russia, Mary Antin divested herself of as much of the past as she could strip away in transforming herself into an American. "I was born, I have lived, and I have been made over," she writes in the opening sentences of her book, and, continuing in this same vein of exultant second birth, "I am just as much out of the way as if I were dead, for I am absolutely other than the person whose story I have to tell." Although only thirty years old at the time she commenced her memoirs, she felt the burdens of the past to be excessive and wanted relief from them. A major reason, perhaps *the* major reason, for writing her book, then, was release from history, more specifically, release from the anguish of the peculiar history of the Jew. "I want to forget," she declares, "sometimes I long to forget. ... It is painful to be consciously of two worlds. The Wandering Jew in me seeks forgetfulness." To jettison the past so as to reach some stasis of identity in a normal, less perplexed present, to weld a unity of self out of the confusions of doubleness—these were the impulses that led Mary Antin to autobiographical invention. The fiction that she allowed herself is a familiar one in our national literature: America as Eden and she, a child of the moment, as Eve newborn in the Garden again.

Despite the fact that the literary sources of this story are Jewish, it is not one that means very much to Jews, perhaps because the story aspects of it, its fictional detachment from the actual nature of Jewish history, are too pronounced. To Jews, that is to say, the Innocence of Eden tends to appear as *mere* fiction, as frail or withered mythology, with the result that this is not a story by which we as Jews come to know very much about ourselves. Nevertheless, it is a central American story, or at least *was* a central American story at the time Mary Antin wrote herself into a new identity, and she obviously felt closely attached to it.

From the vantage point of outward appearances, to withdraw from the obviousness of being Jew so as to become more obviously American can be relatively easy. The changeover began soon after the Antin family arrived in Boston: "With our depised immigrant clothing, we shed also our impossible Hebrew names." Thus Mashke became Mary, and Mary was on her way to becoming just another bright New England girl. Language was to pose a larger obstacle, however, for, more than family name or clothing, it singled out the immigrant and prevented his immediate entrance into American society. English—that is to say, a proper English, untainted by the blemishes of an alien culture—promised a heretofore undreamed-of access to a larger and brighter world, but to attain it, it was felt neccessary to divest oneself of the most glaring badge of foreignness, that jargon of the kitchen and market place, Yiddish. For to maintain Yiddish as an essential language in America was to perpetuate doubleness and, for most immigrants, to be forever incapable of correctness and fluency in the language of their adopted land. The author's father—too old, too European, too obviously Jewish—stood before her as a stammering failure of cultural accommodation, an emblem of a condition that she, of necessity, must herself surpass. One way to do that was to forego or suppress Yiddish, an attainable goal. The public schools would help, as would the settlement houses and the public libraries, to facilitate and encourage the transition into the new language. But most of all there was college, the institution that, more than any other, conferred upon the immigrant fortunate enough to attend certification of literacy at the highest levels, a distinction second only to citizenship itself and, in major ways, its most coveted prize and guarantor.

Reflecting on her college years (she dreamed of attending Radcliffe, the sister school of Harvard, but instead matriculated at New York's Barnard College), Mary Antin writes, with obvious pride in her achievements, "I took all the honors that I deserved; and if I did not learn to write poetry, as I once supposed I should, I learned at least to think in English without an accent." That note of nativist triumph sounds a little harsh and uncanny to our ears today, but there is no reason to doubt the success Mary Antin felt was hers in acquiring a flawless English. With it she grew well beyond her father, who remained, in her description of him, always "hindered by a natural inability to acquire the English language." Her English, honed and polished by her years in college, gave her an image of self that was unambiguously American, and with it she could walk confidently into a future free of the harassments of history. That was her goal, and, from the way her book ends, we are to believe that she accomplished it: "My spirit is not tied to the monumental past, any more than my feet were bound to my grandfather's house below the hill. ... No! it is not I that belong to the past, but the past that belongs to me. America is the youngest of nations...and I am the youngest of America's children."

With that credo of New World affirmation, Polotzk and the life it represented are gone forever, overcome by an act of independent and strikingly American will. Autobiography, in these terms, is equivalent to an act of exorcism: like the Ancient Mariner, Mary Antin would tell her tale to be rid of it. "I will write a bold 'Finis' at the end, and shut the book with a bang!" she resolved. Her bang, our whimper. For the emergence of the new American type in *The Promised Land* meant the submergence of all traditional Jewish life. In Mary Antin's view, America, a liberating land, canceled all the historical claims of the past.

In 1917, five years after the appearance of *The Promised Land,* Abraham Cahan published *The Rise of David Levinsky,* a fictionalized autobiography that once more recounts the passage of an immigrant Jew out of *shtetl* culture and into the broader currents of modern life.[1] Set, in its opening chapters, in the town of Antomir, Russia,

---

[1]For a study of *The Rise of David Levinsky* as fictionalized autobiography, see Ronald Sanders's *The Downtown Jews.* Cahan's expository treatment of his life and times, *Bletter fun mein Leben,* appeared in Yiddish in five volumes, the first two of which

but through most of the narrative in the business world of New York's bustling garment industry, *The Rise of David Levinsky* is another in the long line of American success stories. Yet the weight of Jewish history remains heavy in this book, so heavy, in fact, that it comes to undermine the values of worldly sucess that its protagonist achieves. Although *The Rise of David Levinsky* tells virtually the same story as Mary Antin's book, then, its tone is altogether different. In place of the buoyancy and confidence that accompany Miss Antin's rebirth in America, Cahan's narrative is marked by heavy notes of brooding, depression, puzzlement, and general spiritual malaise.

Why is this so? What, apart from temperamental factors, accounts for the deep ambivalence and ultimate unhappiness of *The Rise of David Levinsky* as against the general optimism and New World cheer of *The Promised Land*? It is not as if David Levinsky fails where Mary Antin succeeds, for he fully makes his way in America and comes to realize the American Dream of rising from poverty to riches. Yet in terms of his basic well-being, his deepest sense of himself, America is not reward enough, and in the end his is a success story fraught with failure, the chronicle of a life torn between opposing dreams.

Obviously America means something else, something *more*, to Mary Antin than it does to Levinsky. To understand why we must travel back to Antomir and Polotzk and consider the different positions that the young David and Mashke occupied in their respective towns; in doing so, we will see that the something *more* that America provided the one derives from the sense of previously having had so much *less*.

The issue is not one of more or less poverty or wealth, for both were poor to a degree difficult for most of us to imagine today. Rather, our concern is with the more classical values of learning and piety, with the traditional Jewish priorities of virtue and the good life. Levinsky, orphaned while still a young boy, devoted himself entirely and passionately to the study of Talmud. His poverty, which was extreme, was eased somewhat by the families who fed and otherwise helped to care for him and who paid him the respect traditionally owing among Jews to a man of religious study. From a worldly standpoint his lot was a miserable one, but the worldly standpoint was not the one by which he measured himself or others

have been abridged and translated as *The Education of Abraham Cahan*; English readers interested in comparing Cahan's fictionalized autobiography with its factual base will want to consult this book.

knew him. Devotional Judaism dictated its own terms of success and stature, and within these terms, Levinsky's life was elevated well beyond the shabby conditions in which he otherwise lived.

Such was not the case with the young Mashke in Polotzk. Mary Antin devotes more than a few pages to recounting the life of *cheder*, a life that she respected but knew only from a distance. "It was not much to be a girl, you see," she writes with noticeable regret. "Girls could not be scholars and rabbonim." There is no reason to doubt her sincerity or the accuracy of her insight when she declares, "There was nothing in what the boys did in cheder that I could not have done—if I had not been a girl." Being a girl, however, she knew that her own instruction was to be found elsewhere: "A girl's real schoolroom was her mother's kitchen."

The discrepancies—some would say the basic inequalities—between these two ways of life cannot be ignored in studying what happened to Jewish life in America. *Di goldene Medinah* glittered to the enterprising David Levinsky in the form of business success, but to a man whose former life had been devoted to the holier business of study and prayer, American success, the piling on of fortune, ultimately proved to be empty. To Mary Antin wealth came in the form of new dreams and opportunities, dreams which Levinsky also coveted but which, in his chase after more than *parnosseh*, he passed up. The Promised Land promised her the chance to at last attend *cheder*, even if *cheder* was now called Barnard College. In America, where no Temple was more revered by the immigrants than College, women were put on an equal footing with men before the fundamental Jewish piety of Learning, and fact that this was a Learning distinct from *lernen* mattered less than the fact that one could liberally partake of it and "improve himself" through study. I suspect that it is no mere coincidence, therefore, that the type of the Intellectual as Hero, which has been greatly furthered, if not originally invented, for American Literature by Jewish writers, and which comes to replace the more traditional Jewish type of the Hero as Pious Man, is prominently established in our literature by a woman.

At least within the early stages of Jewish modernity, in fact, there is probably a close relationship between the feminization of intellect, although, as we shall see a little later in this paper, that correlation is less true today. For now, though, it suffices to note that at a forma-tive stage in American Jewish life, Jewish women were given the chance, virtually for the first time, to occupy themselves seriously with study. And study meant a broader, less restricted world, meant mystery and magical transformations, meant the end of the *shtetl* in its most lackluster aspects and the beginnings of adventure, meant: *America*, a Golden Land. To gain all that even if at the expense of *Yiddishkeit?* To Mary Antin and to countless others like her, both men and women, whose *Yiddishkeit* was a ritualized observance remote from direct contact with "*Toyre*," yes. To a David Levinsky, *Yeshiva bocher* and Talmudist, yes and no.

From the start, Levinsky is acutely sensitive to the fact of his foreign birth ("That I was not born in America was something like a physical defect," he exclaims dejectedly at one point), and he quickly undergoes the familiar process of stripping away the outward appearances of his Jewishness, discarding his traditional European dress and shearing off beard and *payos*. He also labors hard and long to acquire English, which he understands to be a language unique in gesture as well as in vocalization. He is so intent on acquiring distinctively American forms of expressiveness, for instance, that he alters his manner of smoking lest he be discovered "smoking with a foreign accent." Advised by a friend that his English will improve if he reads the Bible, Levinsky undertakes to study the King James Version with the aid of the original Hebrew text, which he reads with fluency and full understanding. He finds, of course, that he can succeed at this odd English lesson, but the magnitude of his cultural inversion, the bizarre phenomenon of a learned Talmudist using *Tanach* as a trot by which to read the English Old Testament, is lost on him. By heart and by training he is no worshipper of foreign gods, yet he is so blinded by his prospects in America ("Success! Success! Success! was the almighty goddess of the hour") that he lets slide his Jewishness and, wittingly or not, comes to bow before the American idol.

Success in American terms is surely his, but Cahan sees clearly enough that David Levinsky's "rise" as a millionaire American businessman entails the "fall" of Levinsky as a Jew. What is more, Levinsky himself comes to acquire this same sad knowledge. "My past and present do not comport well," he exclaims forlornly at the close of the book, and in the confession we recognize the tragedy of Jewish irreconciliation with America.

I have dwelt on these two books at some length because between them they foreshadow and help to chart much of American Jewish writing, and, by implication, much of American Jewish life, during the first half of this century. Over a period of some fifty or sixty years, that is to say, the new Jewish types developed in *The Promised Land* and *The Rise of David Levinsky*—the Jew as liberated, secular intellectual and the Jew as *macher*, or man of influence—emerge as familiar types within American Jewish literature and as types to aspire to within American Jewish society. Needless to say, from the perspective of traditional Judaism there is nothing very Jewish about either type, although by now countless Jews have adapted themselves to one or the other and invested each with something of a distinctively Jewish style. That style—at once intimate and urbane, witty and serious, tender and ironic, an adaptation of the folk qualities of *shtetl* life to the grinding life of large cities—that style will eventually emerge as the hallmark of American Jewish writing and may be its most lasting achievement. But style alone does not suffice to sustain or award significance to the life of such a man as David Levinsky, who, from his first day in America, became aware of what he called "a striking thing": America "was not a world of piety."

To most people, worlds do not rise or fall on the basis of piety, but a Jewish world is inconceivable without it. Following David Levinsky's observation, therefore, we can note another "striking thing": until very recently, almost all of American Jewish writing, reflecting, one imagines, vast stretches of American Jewish life, has been impious. Pieties there have been, of course, in the form of Individualism, Socialism, Art, Intellect, even Alienation, but the classical Jewish pieties have been almost without expression in the writings of American Jewish authors.

The point needs some elaboration, and to illustrate it, I want to consider briefly one of the best known and most cherished of American Jewish autobiographies, Alfred Kazin's *A Walker in the City*. Published for the first time in 1951 and reissued since in several paperback editions, the book has become something of a classic account of the first American-born generation; nevertheless, despite the fact that Kazin's narrative begins in Brownsville and not in Eastern Europe, his story remains the familiar one of escape from the constrictions of *shtetl* life and the discovery of broader, more exciting possibilities beyond. Once more the means of advancement was perceived to lie in language, so that Kazin's story is, among other things, a coming to terms with what many felt to be the awkward fact of Jewish-American bilingualism: the coarse but *heymishdike* Yiddish of kitchen and street in its uneasy mix with the "'refined,' 'correct,' 'nice'" English of the schools. Caught between these two languages—and they were reflective of two distinct worlds—the young Kazin was a stammerer and suffered, as he put it, the "agony" of the "word." The larger, cultural implications of being straddled in this way were not lost on the young boy: "Jews were Jews; Gentiles were Gentiles. The line between them had been drawn for all time."

The rest of this autobiographical narrative can be understood as an effort to dissolve that dividing line and reach some resolution of the conflict of doubleness. Kazin's way, essentially the same as Mary Antin's, was through the pursuit of an intellectual life, although, typically, not a Jewish intellectual life, for *cheder* and *shul* are mentioned only to be rid of them as options. Rather, after an initial flirtation with a wildly romanticized Christianity ("Our own Yeshua ...It was *he*, I thought, who would resolve for me at last the ambiguity and the long ache of being a Jew—Yeshua, our own long-lost Jesus, speaking straight to the mind and heart at once...Yeshua, the most natural of us all, the most direct, the most enchanted"), Kazin made a more permanent and valuable discovery: the public library was a portal through which he could pass to a private, liberating romance with America. "I read as if books would fill my every gap, legitimize my strange quest for the American past, remedy my every flaw, let me in at last into the great world that was anything just out of Brownsville." An impassioned attachment to history and later to literature, but emphatically *not* to Jewish history and literature, was his ticket out of Brownsville and into the promised land beyond.

A Walker in the City is lyric autobiography, a Whitmanesque affirmation of an open, exciting America, and a hymn to the private life that perhaps only such an America can provide. It is a celebratory work, rich in cadence, ultimately expansive in mood, and alive with the expectations of adventure beyond. "Beyond," in fact, is its favorite, most frequently repeated word, and signals the major directions of Kazin's intellectual and spiritual quest: *beyond* Brownsville, *beyond* the family home, *beyond* Hebrew school and synagogue, and into the World. Despite the fact that *A Walker in the City* has become canonized as a central text of American Jewish writing, therefore, it is really an end-of-the-road book, a farewell to Jewish life. To be sure, the book begins as a *return* to Brownsville, but a return enacted only to register a last goodbye. One can still quicken to the rich sociological representations of *Yiddishkeit* in *A Walker in the City*, to the ample sights and sounds and smells of an American *shtetl*, but otherwise this is a book fundamentally lacking in Jewish interest. Its pieties are those of the Romantic tradition, as there were localized in America by Emerson and Whitman, some of whose descendants, strangely enough, were born in places like Polotzk and Brownsville.

Were our story to end here—and only a few years ago the signs were that it might end here—we would be led to believe that traditional Jewish life and the values of life in America do not easily reconcile. At least as depicted by representative American autobiographies, the passage from *shtetl* culture into the broader streams of American modernity almost inevitably had to be at the expense of Jewishness. Jewish culture was a thing easier to discard than to maintain and, when confronted by the allure of possibilities in America, Jewish culture could not successfully compete for the primary energies and loyalties, the major work of mind and spirit, of the immigrant generation and its immediate offspring. The result has been an abandonment of the major loci of Jewish life—home, *shul*, and school—and their replacement by other spheres of influence and activity.

The role of language in this transition (a more optimistic reading might prefer to call it "transposition") is a vital one and needs to be looked at more closely. Jewish culture is transmitted, linguistically and otherwise, within the three major spheres mentioned above. Home, *shul*, and school are intimate with one another in Jewish life and, as overlapping or concentric circles, largely comprise it. Just as it is all but impossible to imagine a Jewish life devoid of family, study, and prayer, so too is it virtually inconceivable to maintain family, engage in study, and pray altogether outside of Jewish languages. The primary vehicle for the transmission of culture is always language, and Jewish culture is dependent on its own historic language, chiefly Hebrew but also, for the majority of Jews who emigrated to America, Yiddish.

As we have seen from the books that have been considered so far, however, Hebrew and Yiddish both give way in America to a passion for English as an absolute language. Here, for instance, is

Mary Antin's view on the subject:

> I am glad, most of all, that the Americans began by being Englishmen, for thus did I come to inherit this beautiful language in which I think. It seems to me that in any other language happiness is not so sweet, logic is not so clear. I am not sure that I could believe in my neighbors as I do if I thought about them in un-English words. I could almost say that my conviction of immortality is bound up with the English of its promise.

And here is Alfred Kazin, in church:

> The chief impression that it [a Christian church that he had wandered into] made on me, who expected all Christians to be as fantastic as albinos, was that these people were not, apparently, so completely different from us as I had imagined. I was bewildered. What really held me there was the number of things written in English. I had associated God only with a foreign language. Suspended from the ceiling over the altar was a great gold-wood sign on which the black Gothic letters read: I AM THE RESURRECTION AND THE LIFE.

As for David Levinsky, we have already observed him laboriously translating the English of the King James Version back into the Hebrew of *Tanach.*

The close connection between English and Christianity in each of these three instances is obvious and requires no intricate analysis. It may suffice to quote Arthur Hertzberg, who recently has had some interesting things to say about this connection:

> All of us who write in English go, so to speak, against the grain of the language. When you write in English a fairly substantial amount of the language has within it its own Christian past. ... Hebrew, a derivative of ancient Semitic, had to overcome its pagan past. But it did. By the same token, any serious Jewish writing in English has to overcome the Christian past of the language.

Hertzberg emphasizes that he is not excluding Jews from writing in English but only alerting them to problems that occur when they use a language they themselves have not fashioned. Admittedly, it is easier to assert than to prove the connections and discrepancies between languages and specific cultures, but writers themselves feel these links and gaps sharply. "How," asks Hertzberg, by way of illustration, "do you translate *tzadik* into English? Saint?" Or, to cite an example from Yiddish, we recall Maurice Samuel's homier instance of such cultural differentials as *kugl* being no more "pudding" than *shoyfer* is "ram's horn," although both find their lexical equivalents in those terms.

Abraham Cahan asked himself such questions as these when he wrote *The Rise of David Levinsky* and worked out his answers through the use of rough English approximations of the Hebrew and Yiddish words that came first to mind. Thus when he wants his narrator to refer to an *amoretz*, he calls him an "ignorant 'man of the earth'"; when he wants to describe a *Simchas Torah* celebration, he writes of that "day of picturesque merrymaking and ceremony," the "Rejoicing of the Law"; and when he wants to wish a close friend "*l'chayim*," he raises his glass and exclaims, "Here is good health, Gitelson." Now Cahan knew that no Gitelson was ever toasted in such a way, but he also knew that his protagonist, intent as he was on reinventing himself as an American, probably would mouth such pale affectations as these. For to Levinsky, as to Mary Antin, "people who were born to speak English were superior beings." "Even among fallen women," Levinsky, a sometime visitor to brothels, declares, "I would seek those who were real Americans." As a real American would say, why settle for less than *mameshdike skhoyre?*

Without belaboring the point, and without even being able to support it conclusively, one feels certain of the connections between historic cultures and the languages in which they are rooted. Languages have their own logic, and they structure our thoughts and feelings, the basic tenor and weight of our experience, in distinct ways. Inasmuch as Jewish experience grows out of and requires its own language, Hebrew and, within the history of Ashkenazic Jewry, Yiddish have been basic.

Now, without attempting to draw direct cause-and-effect relationships, it needs to be observed that the diminished state of Hebrew and Yiddish within the major life of American Jewry, itself largely an extension of Ashkenazic culture, has been accompanied by a general weakening of the cultural forces of traditional Judaism. In a society where home life is not notably strong, the Jewish family has held up better than most, but even a casual reader of the literature produced by American Jewish authors is aware of the typical reduced pattern of the Jewish home: the shrunken or absent father; the omnipresent, domineering, ludicrous mother; and children who can neither easily abide nor fully abandon the parents whom they simultaneously love and hate. Much of this has by now become mere caricature, a bad joke that refuses to go away, but certainly the novelists have captured a piece of the truth. As for the literary representations of *shul* and *cheder*, a sadder truth applies: they are either missing altogether or appear as brief, distasteful episodes in the lives of children, who will leave them behind with their Bar Mitzvah pledges to continue the study and observance of Judaism. What remains and continues to carry much of American Jewish writing is style and sociology, neither of which knows anything of the Covenant the Jews have with God and history.

The Jew's reinvention of himself as an American, therefore, has tended to create a complex new creature, both more enriched and more deprived than his former self. He is now monolingual where he had been bilingual; is neither altogether without a history nor in possession of one; has largely removed himself from the devotional life of the past to assume, without fully knowing their value, the debts and duties of a secularized present; and is on the whole bemused, ambivalent, and ironic about the intertwinings of success and failure he knows as citizen, neighbor, intellectual, businessman, lover, anxious parent, harried daughter, or hounded son. The largest questions that face him are the ones framed by David Levinsky, his major prototype, half a century ago: "Who am I?" and "Who am I living for?" His answers most often also seem to be some form of Levinsky's: "I am lonely ... [and] feel the deadly silence of solitude. ...My present station, power, the amount of worldly happiness at my command, and the rest of it, seem to be devoid of significance."

It is at this point, admittedly a low one, that our story becomes suddenly complicated and interesting in unexpected ways. Irving Howe helps to sound the note for it in his "Memoir of the Thirties" (collected in *Steady Work*), a decade that, in its implications for the future, is only now, perhaps, beginning to be adequately understood:

> In the thirties...Jewishness was not something one had much choice about. ... What you believed, or said you believed, did not matter nearly as much as what you were. ... The forces that shaped one, the subtle enveloping conditions that slowly did their work on character and disposition, were not really matters of choice. The world I never made, made me.

Howe, a literary and culture critic with an eye especially well trained on the historical moment, gives us, in the passage just cited, the antithetical—he might say, not at all abjectly, "old-fashioned"—

view of our subject. History had begun to swirl once again in the thirties, and the Jew, as always, was about to get doused. As always, though—and in this hesitancy Jewish history touches bottom, decends to its tragic dimensions—the Jew was only half-aware of the storms about to sweep over him. Today, from the safety of distance, it is possible to see what was taking place in the earlier decades of this century, to see, in Howe's exact description of it, how the world of the Jews was being shaped, or misshaped, by forces stronger and less benevolent than that of the private will. This new awareness has sent a shudder through more recent Jewish writing, has awakened it to history in ways it previously had not been awake, and, in terms of autobiographical writing, has introduced a strain of revisionism. For to be conscious of history and of the Jew's vulnerability to it, including its worst excesses, is to render any belief in the shaping power of private imagination much less tenable, much less serious. The result—although not the immediate result, for the time lag between the press of event and literature's recording of it is often considerable—has been a literature of new Jewish self-awareness, a winding back from the outer limits of acculturation and accommodation to points closer to the inner sources of historical Jewishness.

In looking at this literature, I choose to limit myself, as before, to a consideration of selected autobiographical works, acknowledging that there are other texts and even other kinds of data that might be equally appropriate for such a study as this one. I choose autobiographies, however, for they are the most self-conscious of the literary forms, the most unmediated declartions of self and, as such, provide, when honestly written, as detailed a scrutiny of the exposed self as we are likely to get.

One such text, exposed to the point of embarrassment, is Norman Podhoretz's *Making It*. The book was criticized by certain of its readers upon its publication in 1967 as being brash and tasteless, an exhibition of the "pushy" Jew at his most excessive. Excess, indeed, is a quality of Podhoretz's autobiography, for in this book we have a coming together of *both* of the cultural archetypes alluded to earlier: the Jew as intellectual and the Jew as *macher*. Podhoretz set about to integrate the two, to show in abundant detail how Money, Power, and Fame might attach themselves to the intellectual life. A very American thing to do, getting the mind to pay off, and an enterprise that can be traced back in American literature at least as far as Benjamin Franklin, whose *Autobiogrpahy*, among the most celebrated in our national letters, is in innocent ways a prototype of Podhoretz's. What shocked or "offended" in *Making It*, therefore, was not the success story *per se* but the terms in which that story was spelled out, namely the style and sociology of its telling. These, the prominent Jewish components of the book, together with the author's "brag" about making it, generated the uneasy feelings of an excessive self-exposure.

The Jewishness of *Making It* extends well beyond the account of the evolution of an intellectual *macher*, however, and has not been sufficiently appreciated to date. I refer to the fact that with Podhoretz we begin to see an alternative to the Jew as *merely* secular intellectual and catch glimpses of something more, of options within the intellectual life that permit and encourage a return to Jewishness while fully maintaining a stake in the world. The uniqueness, and perhaps also the attractive power, of Podhoretz's account of his career derive from the fact that he did achieve a certain intellectual success without having to abandon his connections to Jewish sources. He was not the first to do so, of course, for prior to Podhoretz we have the examples of Maurice Samuel and, as a more complicated case, Ludwig Lewisohn,[2] but in his own generation, which is to say among those born in America, Podhoretz is among the first to show us the affinities, rather than the inevitable separations, between intellectual and Jew, or, in keeping within the more localized terms of the book, between Columbia College and the Jewish Theological Seminary. In one's journey from Brownsville to Manhattan, then, one could take along a Jewish book or two, even if these were not judged to be the equal of John Donne or T. S. Eliot. In brief, the Gentleman and the Jew were not altogether irreconcilable. In showing their compatability—even if a bit self-consciously, a bit too aggressively—Podhoretz helped to bring about a necessary modification in the Jewish intellectual's self-image. With him, the problems that nagged at the

---

[2] A more comprehensive study of Jewish autobiographers in America would, of necessity, have to include more detailed attention to these two writers than is possible in the present essay; of special note are Maurice Samuel's *Little Did I Know* and Ludwig Lewisohn's *Upstream*. Although both writers came into their own as far back as the 1920's, they nonetheless can find a place in the later development of American Jewish writing, much of which they presage in their own careers.

young Alfred Kazin—"Why were these people *here*, and we *there*? Why had I always to think of insider and outsider, of their belonging and our not belonging?"—begin to drop away.

Podhoretz can also be credited with being among the first to appreciate the breakthrough that Saul Bellow had begun to accomplish in American fiction. Without any of the intimidations of an excessive self-awareness, indeed with gusto and at full imaginative strength, Bellow, starting with *The Adventures of Augie March*, began to construct a prose style that, in Podhoretz's description of it, "crossed the regnant 'high' literary language...with American Jewish colloquial." That style had been attempted by others and has since become something of a plaything in the hands of lesser writers, but Bellow was the first who could *think* in it, naturally and deeply, encompassing in authentic tones the mixed life, Yiddish-American, of Jews in America's big cities. The result has been the beginning of a new and fully legitimate literary language, extended in *Herzog* and *Mr. Sammler's Planet* and still supple enough for further extensions and discoveries beyond.

This turn to a new literary language, a *Jewish* literary language, if you will, is a highly positive development and has been accompanied by related developments elsewhere in the literary culture of American Jews. Most significantly, there has been an effort to locate and perhaps make accessible to contemporary Jewish experience the language of an authentic Jewish past. The odds against this effort succeeding are formidable, but so too is the passion to succeed, at least on the part of that small but admirable group of scholars and writers who are laboring at the task of recovery and revival. I look to Irving Howe once more to provide the historical frame for our subject:

> We were living directly after the Holocaust of the European Jews.
> We might scorn our origins; we might crush America with discoveries
> of ardor; we might change our names. But we knew that but for an
> accident of geography we might also now be bars of soap. At least
> some of us could not help feeling that in our earlier claims to have
> shaken off all ethnic distinctiveness there had been something false,
> something shaming. Our Jewishness might have no clear religious or
> national content, it might be helpless before the criticism of believers;
> but Jews we were, like it or not, and liked or not. ("The New York
> Intellectuals," collected in *Decline of the New*)

American Jewish writers are criticized on occasion for ignoring the Holocaust, and, if one is to measure the quality of their work or even of their caring, by the number and quality of their books on the subject of the Nazi destruction of the European Jewish communities, the criticism might be borne out. There are a few novels, a play or two, some minor poems, but on the whole American writers have not contributed much to international Holocaust literature. What they have done, or what a few have done, Howe himself prominent among them, is effect a return to Yiddish, a return that must be judged against the background of the Holocaust and may be deemed an authentic and powerful response to it.

Everyone who touches Yiddish today, as scholar or writer, is aware that he is in communion with the dead, just as every such scholar or writer refuses to acknowledge the death as total or permanent. As a result, every striving to maintain or revive life for Yiddish can be judged an authentic act of Jewish piety, to some perhaps the only such enactment still possible. No one looks for a new messiah of language to arise and do for Yiddish what Ben Yehuda did for Hebrew, but quietly and modestly the work of memorialization, recovery, and nascent revival goes on. Howe's own contribution to this effort—as co-editor of three major anthologies of Yiddish literature in translation, as co-editor of the recently released edition of Peretz stories, and as occasional essayist—has been substantial. Almost certain to be equally substantial, and integral with the ties that American Jewish culture has with Yiddish, will be Howe's long-awaited memoir and history, "The World of Our Fathers." To some, and I suspect that Howe is among them, the Jewish Covenant has been transferred from the realm of theology to that of language, with *mame-loshn* validated as a new *loshn koydesh*. To these, the Commanding Voice of Auschwitz, as Emil Fackenheim has designated the compelling force of the Holocaust on Jewish devotional life, calls across the void in Yiddish.

This connection to Yiddish, which is not to be confused with or reduced to the vogue of nostalgia for "the joys of being Jewish," is, for some, the manifestation of a will towards Jewishness that may find its expression nowhere else, or at least nowhere else so strongly. One sees it again—once in intimate connection to Yiddish, once still groping for its language—in the autobiographies of Ronald Sanders and Herbert Gold, the last I shall be considering here.

Both can be viewed as acts of homage to "worlds of our fathers," although, as we shall see, two very different kinds of fathers are involved. Both are attempts to think through a personal identity through the recollection of historical ties, which must begin, of course, with family history. To acknowledge oneself the son of his father should be the most natural and commonplace of admissions, but, as we have seen, the reverse more typically has been the case: American Jewish writing, as most of modern literature in general, prefers to see itself as unsired. Sander's *Reflections on a Teapot* (1972) and Gold's *Fathers* (1966), by restoring the father to a position of centrality, registered what may be a sizeable advance, therefore, one that entered fiction as well, and at about the same time, in the last two novels of Saul Bellow. If, indeed, these are not mere isolated instances but speak for a more widely shared reconciliation, American Jewish writing may be about to come into a period of new maturity. There is hardly anything it needs more and hardly a better way to begin to achieve it than through a retrieval of the father; without it, the writing is doomed to remain forever willful, solipsistic, incapable of taking up any serious stance before the public pressures of history and the private dread of death. A recovery of the father affords at least the possibilities of an opening out to history, of *learning* something beyond the pleasures and pains of ego. Such a literature would be on the way to developing a character that is fundamentally Jewish, if for no other reason than for its reversal of the emphasis on Son-ship that began with Christianity and remains dominant still today. "Through the son shall you know the father" is not Jewish creed; an acknowledgment of the priority, if not the ultimate authority, of the father, and through him of whatever extensions and continuities there are that lie beyond the limits of the isolated self, is.

Something of this latter position, secularized to be sure but still tenaciously Jewish, forms the basis of Ronald Sanders's autobiography. It is all the more remarkable, perhaps, because the elder Sanders was an Englishman who was fond of Jews and had close associations with them but was not himself Jewish. His wife, the author's mother, was, and yet *Reflections on a Teapot* is less her story than it is his. *Halakhic* definitions of Jewishness aside (and I set them aside only because they seem to have played no major role in the young Sanders's sense of what bestowed a significant Jewish identity on him), cultural descent in this book is from the father, not the mother.

Sanders's story, like Kazin's and Podhoretz's, charts the road, more cultural than geographic, that takes a bright young man—"the Jew as America's ultimate English major," as Sanders calls him—from Brooklyn to Manhattan, which means from the common ground of an American *shtetl* to one of the elevated summits of the literary life. More so than with these two of his precursors, who early on conceived of the literary life as an attainment of high culture, Sanders spent his early years in the more typical American way, that is to say in "pop" culture, so the *Reflections on a Teapot* is, among other things, a detailed chronicle of growing up amid comic books, the music hall, the movies, radio, athletics, and other such popular amusements. Still, college is in the picture, in the form of Kenyon during the time of John Crowe Ransom, and the shapings of a literary intellectual begin to take place.

And then an unexpected turn, away from the reigning literary aestheticism and towards "a place where some of my roots lay," a turn to history. But *where* in history, and what kind of intellectual equipment could a Kenyon College English major bring to the study of history? The answers once more were to be found in language, more particularly—and irony of ironies—in Yiddish:

> I *wanted* to learn Yiddish. I wanted to so much, in fact, that I wondered if the entire process by which I had arrived at a thesis topic [Sanders chose to write on Abraham Cahan, whose David Levinsky labored so hard to detach himself *from* Yiddish] had not been unconsciouly guided by this desire. Yiddish, the comic-pathetic vehicle of some kind of truth about myself and my origins. ...

The immediate result of the study of Yiddish was *The Downtown Jews*, Sanders's intellectual and cultural history of Abraham Cahan and the whole Lower East Side world of *The Rise of David Levinsky*. The longer term result was this:

> I was beginning to like my scholarly career now that it had taken on a Jewish tinge. For the first time in my life, I got into the habit of thinking of myself as a Jewish intellectual at all times, and the world took on new meaning for me as a result.

Yiddish, "the voice of some lost or dying authenticity," reconciled Sanders to a past he had craved but never owned. As the language "of the mid-century disaster suffered by the Jewish people," it anchored him in history and turned him in two directions: toward Israel, where, in the view from Masada, he recognized a piece of his future, and toward the immigrant culture of the Lower East Side, where he recognized a coveted but withheld piece of his past. The language embodied a history whose voice he resolved to hear echoing in his own, "the,voice of my Russian-Jewish grandparents who had died before I was born." In straining to hear that silenced past, he reconstituted a future for himself. Just as the flight from Yiddish earlier in the century meant a flight from a Jewish world, so, too, at mid-century did a return to Yiddish help effect the retrieval— in Sanders's case, perhaps even the invention—of Jewishness.

A comparable turn is observable, although it is without the benefit of as fully mediating a language, and hence is more tentative, more preliminary, in Herbert Gold's last two books. *Fathers*, a novel written in the form of a memoir, was followed in 1972 by *My Last Two Thousand Years*, a memoir written in the form of a novel. The two together comprise an informal autobiography and attest to an astonishing reversal of attitude about Jewish history and the individual's place within it. For only ten years previously, in *Commentary's* Symposium on "Jewishness and the Younger Intellectuals," Gold could forecast that "chicken soup and Yiddish jokes will tarry awhile. But the history of the Jews from now on will be one with the history of everybody else." By the time of *My Last Two Thousand Years*, he was affirming that "necessary connection to the past that we all need to survive" and confessing his desire "to be continuous" with Jewish life. What had happened in those ten years to effect that kind of reversal? And had it happened, was it happening *still*, to more than just Gold alone?

The personal element can be accounted for easily enough. Gold, always a prolific writer, had come into his own as a novelist and was beginning to enjoy the rewards of his success, but like Levinsky before him, he was discovering that success American style—a modern man, Gold adds Girls to Money, Power, and Fame—did not satisfy him. It did not because it could not answer to his needs to feel part of a particular community of men. "What is a Jew and why am I this thing?" was the irrepressible but unanswerable question that shadowed his success and turned it sour. The result, as recorded in his memoirs, was spiritual nausea, a turning away from the satieties of success and a turning against the self: "I hated my life." From this point on the interests of *My Last Two Thousand Years* are twofold: as a critique of the literary life and with it most of the values of cultural Modernism, and as a discovery of a more central identity through an awakening to history. In his role as critic, Gold is as strong in his judgments *against* careerism in writing and the general commerce of culture as previous literary intellectuals have been avid for these. Having made it as a writer, he knows what literary success in America means, and also what it cannot possibly mean: "Literature is not a nation or a religion." In quest of national and religious ties he has to seek elsewhere—in Europe, where he finds among stray survivors of Hitler the strength of Jewish will, and in Israel, where Jewish will manifests itself to him in the restoration of nationhood and the revival of religious possibilities. These encounters with Jews, unremarkable in themselves, teach Gold a simple but longed-for truth: "I was moved by my kind." His encounter with Israel, made poignant by his being in Jerusalem at the time of a *Yom Ha'atzmaut* celebration, delivered another truth, one that might be gained for a Jew only in Israel: "History and the celebrators of history were contemporary with one another." Finally, during a quiet moment of reflection in the Judean hills, a long-delayed encounter with himself: "My fate," writes Gold, "was to become what I was born to be."

A beginning, no more than that, but a significant beginning, one that turns a man to history and, through history, returns him to himself. But only to begin once more, for, as Gold readily admits, he has had only a glimpse, albeit a transforming one, of what his destiny as a Jew is to mean, and he knows that he must come to know "more than [he has] thus far told." That requires language, a language that will give proper names to the aura of history that he has discovered within himself and make possible some equivalent discovery without. Sanders, essentially a historian, took the historian's way and searched out a past for himself through Yiddish, later also adding Hebrew; that past guarantees him a present and, as long as he remains faithfully within these languages, awards him a future as well. Gold, an imaginative writer in search of narrative means, has had intimations of a future but, lacking a way into the language of the past, stands still before an articulate present, that is to say a present continuous with history. That is what he so badly wants and needs, as his last two books persuasively argue, but the argument is almost wholly on the level of will.

American Jewish writing, or at least the particularist strain of it that I have been trying to trace out in this essay, is poised right there, at the cutting edge of will. It is both starting point and stopping point, for although it signifies a direction, it is, by itself, helpless to follow it out. Language, the writer's means of implementing will, has been lacking for too long; or, rather, it has been serving the will of other masters; for want of a more precise name, we shall say it has been serving the Will of the Imagination.

The Will of the Imagination is a powerful and seductive one, but it is not Jewish Will. It knows nothing of history and cares nothing for the Lord of History. Indeed, it has declared history void of a Master and has arrogated to itself the sole powers of Creation. Its only piety is pleasure, its only wish, to be indulged. Indulge Imagination and you can have what you will—the riches of magic and mystery, the transforming powers of illusion, the obliteration of all precedence and priority, a momentary triumph over conscience, sense, and time. Omnipotent Imagination craves to be indulged and courts indulgence through the wiles of Romance—gently, teasingly tempered for some, passionate and orgiastic for others. It is a Goddess who has waged war against and conquered its God, who gave up Wisdom for Pleasure and, sated now beyond the point of recovery, has relinquished all Authority in this world and in any world to come.

That is why Imagination, Supreme Pagan Lady that she is, can only be countered by Another Woman, one who knows her ways, is equal to her charms, one who has been raised on her loveliest poetry and hence will not succumb to the reigning powers of her speech. The match, as all such matches, is for the God; and it will take place, as all such matches must, in the arena of language.

The Other Lady is a Jew, and that promises to make the match especially interesting. Ultimately, it may also prove to make it uneven, for she is something of a new Jew—call her a New Traditionalist, if you will—born in America but a claimant to the best of Old as well as New World Culture, one who has drunk deep at the waters of Imagination and now returned to more Biblical wells. Both College and *cheder* are hers, therefore, the knowledge of the Goddess and the knowledge of the God. And therein lies a power not known before, neither by those who abandoned *cheder* for College nor by those whose learning embraced the Goddess but never knew the God.

The result may be a language to implement Jewish will as it now exists in America, a language that will blend the two worlds of Learning and *lernen*, Poetry and Torah. Those are startling combinations, never before fully achieved by an American writer. Saul Bellow, especially the Bellow of *Herzog* and *Mr. Sammler's Planet*, has come as close as anyone has to developing such a language, but both of his last two novels, brilliant as they are, show a still lingering irreconciliation with the Lady. She is overcome, it is true, but by men who still half-lament her passing and who themselves cannot reveal the God who will assume her place.

No, her major challenge will come from a woman, a Jewish Woman, and therein lies a pleasing twist to our story. Within traditional Judaism, to aspire to the condition of intellect, intellect conceived as in the service of piety, has been to aspire to the masculine condition, heretofore an all but impossible, because unrealizable, goal for women. Feminine piety within Judaism consequently has been nonintellectual, with the result that Jewish women have had either to restrain the urgings of intellect or look outside of the tradition to satisfy them. The result of that, as noted earlier, has been a coalescence within Judaism of secularization and feminization, the twin components of romantic adoration.

Just when or even why that situation began to change, I do not know, but the fact that there has been a change is made emphatic by the presence of a woman as our most forceful writer. The one writer in America today most alert to, because most anguished by, the problems under discussion here — the conflicting claims of learning and *lernen*, of Imaginative and Jewish will — is Cynthia Ozick. She is also the writer most committed to finding a language that will resolve the conflict creatively. She calls it New Yiddish, a language centrally Jewish in its concerns, touched by the covenant and attentive to its commands while remaining still fully expressive of life in the world. With Cynthia Ozick, Jewish will and the literary means to give it expression stand at the point described by Franz Rosenzweig half a century ago. That it has taken us this long to catch up to him is not to our credit:

> A new 'learning' is about to be born — rather, it has been born. It is a learning in reverse order. A learning that no longer starts from the Torah and leads into life, but the other way round: from life, from a world that knows nothing of the Law, or pretends to know nothing, back to the Torah. That is the sign of the time.

It is the sign of the time because it is the mark of the men of the time.
...All of us to whom Judaism, to whom being a Jew, has again become
the pivot of our lives...know that in being Jews we must not give up
anything, not renounce anything, but lead everything back to Judaism.
From the periphery back to the center; from the outside, in.

The Personal Life Deeply Lived

by Anaïs Nin

It was, of course, because I suspected the accuracy of memory that from the age of eleven on I made such a careful recording day by day of everything I heard and saw. I really felt that memory interfered and intercepted and distorted experience, that everything was rearranged and reordered in terms of what we are today. And I wanted to see a development of life, the growth and development of experience in terms of a continuous evolution, observing all its transformations. Watching a person grow, watching a writer grow, and watching an artist grow, as I did so carefully and with such minute intensity, made me aware that memory was treacherous and that this instantaneous portrait contained an element which was left out of memoirs and certainly out of fiction. As D. H. Lawrence once said, the greatest problem of fiction was how to transport the living essence, the living quality of experience into a prearranged art form, and the danger in this transposition, this carrying of experience into fiction, was that it might die in the process. Now in the diary, no such death takes place because there is no distance. The living moment is caught, and in catching this by accumulation and by accretion a personality emerges in all its ambivalences, contradictions, and paradoxes, and finally in its most living form.

In Europe the diary form was very respected. Every writer had a diary; the diary seemed to be a part of the development of the writer. We never looked on it as a purely subjective occupation; it was part of the literary life, it was a cultural contribution. Amiel, Gide,

George Sand, and Virginia Woolf—all our writers kept diaries. But in America we have had very few. American tradition has not encouraged diary writing. But now we are taking it up with a different purpose; we're taking it up as an instrument for knowing ourselves, for creating ourselves.

Today, diaries are being taken more seriously. There is a group of young future psychoanalysts who were given diaries to write as part of their training. After six weeks they sent for me, and they said that they were absolutely petrified with fear. I said: "How can you be? You are men who are dealing all the time with all the complexities of human nature; you're psychologists, you're going to deal with all the difficulties and problems of human behavior. How can you be afraid?" They said: "Well, we used to talk about all these problems in groups, but we never sat alone in a room with a blank book and had to face ourselves." They were mature, but they were afraid.

Now this fear is also very natural because we have grown up with the idea of an eye looking over our shoulder. Either it is the eye of the parent, or the eye of the teacher, or even in some cases they said God could see everything that we did. Those terrors of being watched are part of our childhood, and they are certainly based on fact. And this very idea of being watched by the world is what makes it necessary for us to turn to a secret occupation where we can really confront ourslves without the sense of the world watching. We have lived with too much consciousness of the rest of the world watching. us. We think it is always a virtue, but it's not a virtue when it prevents us from being truthful or when it prevents us from developing ourselves.

Now the value of the secret is that we are never quite sincere if we are writing something which we think someone is going to read. The necessary condition is that it has to be a secret. I matured enough to feel that my diary no longer needed to be a secret, but the very condition of it was the fact that I didn't think anyone would read it, and therefore I was utterly sincere with myself. Also it helped me to make the separation between my real self and the role-playing a woman is called upon to do. The roles which were imposed on me as a woman by my culture—from two different cultures, the Latin and then later the American—I fulfilled. I did what I called my duty. But at the same time the diary kept my other self alive, it showed what I really wanted, what I really felt, what I really thought.

So the reason I believe in this so much and can talk about it now so fervently is that it was my own discovery. By gradually building up this shelter of the diary, I built a place where I could always tell the truth, where I could paint my friends truthfully, where I could maintain the vacillating phases of relationship which baffle us sometimes and from which we would sometimes like to run away. The diary obliged me to stay there, to stay whole, and to continue to feel. I had to tell the diary everything. I could not afford to drop out; I could not afford to become insensible, because then I would have had nothing to tell to the diary.

Humorous things happen too. There is an incentive to make your life interesting, so that your diary will not be dull. We used to talk sometimes about that. There is a period, in the third *Diary*, I recall, when I say: "What is happening? I really haven't anything very interesting to say, and I must do something about it. Really this is my fault, this is my life to create." This creation of expression, you see then, is tied to the creation of one's life itself.

So it's very essential, this pursuit of the inner world, and don't let anyone say that it is a selfish occupation or that it is a narcissistic one. One critic, Leon Edel, said that the *Diary* was nothing but a narcissus pool. To which I replied: "I have never seen a narcissus pool in which a thousand characters appeared at the same time." This is absolutely true; as a matter of fact, I counted them! But our culture has a suspicion of what people do when they turn inward. The fear was probably that they would turn inward, as if inside a sea shell and never come out again. Well, sometimes we have good reasons for not coming out. But I found that I did come out the other end, that the sea shell has an opening.

I attribute to my diary this faculty for receiving others, for being prepared to receive the face or the voice, the presence, the words of others. It's a form of loving, it's a form of attentiveness. And when sometimes the students say to me: "Of course, you knew so many famous people," I say: "Don't forget they were not famous at all when we first knew each other; we were accidentally thrown together and none of us had done anything; we chose each other finally for genuine reasons, for potentials in each other." We were not finished writers, were not famous writers; we were just like students sitting next to each other. But we paid attention to the one who was next to us. We didn't seek the famous writers in France. We simply encouraged each other and made our own growth. So we learned to live with others, to help others be creative, to help others achieve their work. We were very encouraging, very fraternal. And then, of course, inevitably everything I heard I would put down. It's like those little Japanese flowers that you put in water. I would finally learn to let it come in full bloom. Instead of being hasty about the descriptions, I wanted to go deeper and deeper and deeper.

At this time, when we live such an accelerated life, when we think that contacts are very transient and passing and superficial, then more than ever we have to examine the fears we have about revealing ourselves. Part of this fear found its expression in the novel. Nevertheless, women continued to write diaries and we know that George Sand, even though she produced so many novels, felt it necessary to keep a diary in which she told about her own life.

So the secrecy that I kept for so many years, until the time that I decided to share the diaries with you, revealed something to me that I think applies to all of us. It revealed the fear we have of exposing our deepest self, and it is this fear which has played a major role in what we call the alienated society. I don't think it comes from the external cause, the transience of American life, the fact that we move about, the fact that we are easily uprooted. For the fact that I was uprooted is exactly what made me turn once more to writing.

When I came to America I couldn't speak the language, and I had no friends. So the diary became the friend and the father confessor. It was also the substitute for the absent father. And it was in this way that I learned the vital quality of what seemed to be a monologue, an interior monologue. For it wasn't only that. It was the way I was going to rebuild the bridge that was broken by the separation of my parents and by the uprooting to a foreign country. So the writing began to have a living, vital meaning which had nothing to do with literature. The diary became not only a companion, so that I wouldn't be lost in a foreign country with a language I couldn't speak, but also a source of contact with myself. It was a place where I could tell the truth and where I felt that nobody would look.

Now this habit which I acquired accidentally as the result of a psychic trauma became a guiding element in my life and took on a different color after awhile. It was not only the story of myself but of the adventure of coming to a new country. It became the diary of an adventurer. It made me look at my life, at sorrowful moments, at moments of great disintegrating experiences, and constantly reminded me that it was an adventure, that it was a tale. Somehow the transference into writing gave it just that little bit of space which I needed to sustain the painful part of the experience. So there were always those two guiding objectives. One was growth, watching my own growth; and then, in watching my own growth it naturally follows that I watched and observed the growth of others around me. So your attentiveness, your care for what is happening, your watchfulness, your meditation on what happens, your examination of what happens, the fact that you are observing others and that you are not only writing down your life but that you are also naturally concerned with the growth of people around you, make that a necessary part of our existence. Because what we don't write down often remains rather nebulous in our feelings. And at this moment, particularly when women are trying really to find their identity, I found that the thing most lacking was this power of expression of what you feel in a certain situation, what you think, what you believe, which you want to impart to others.

Tonight I was asked to talk about writing, not writing as literature but writing as intimately connected with our lives—I would even say as necessary to our lives. ...And now I want to tell you, from the very beginning, how this writing happened to become for me so linked with life and how it was a necessary part of living. When I was nine years old a doctor made an erroneous diagnosis and said I would never walk again. My first reaction then was to ask for pencil and paper and to start making portraits of the members of my family. Then this continued in the form of notes which I gathered in a little notebook and even wrote on it "Member of the French Academy." Quite obviously there was then a turning to writing as a way of life because I thought I was going to be deprived of the normal activities of a child or an adolescent. But I'm trying to use this as an example of the importance of writing as a way of learning to live; for when I was able to walk again and there was no question of that impediment, the writing remained a source of contact with myself and with others.

It's also very symbolic that when I was asked once to go to a masquerade in which we had to dress as our madness, I put my head in a bird cage. And coming out of the bird cage was a sort of ticker tape of the unconscious, long strips of paper on which I had copied a great deal of writing. This was, of course, a very clear symbol of how I hoped to escape from my cage.

You might say, however, when you are reading the *Diary* now: "Oh well, it was easy for you, you could write well." But I want you to know that at twenty I wrote very badly, and I purposely gave my first novel to the library of Northwestern University so that students could see the difference between the writing I did at twenty and the writing I do now. The mistake we make when we choose a model is that we choose the point of arrival. We are unaware of the things that have been overcome, like shyness, or not being able to speak in public (I couldn't even speak to the people I knew). The final achievements are what we notice and then say: "Well it's no use modelling ourselves after this or that writer because we don't have these particular gifts." I didn't have any particular gift in my twenties. I didn't have any exceptional qualities. It was the persistence and the great love of my craft which finally became a discipline, which finally made me a craftsman and a writer.

The only reason I finally was able to say exactly what I felt was because, like a pianist practising, I wrote every day. There was no more than that. There was no studying of writing, there was no literary discipline, there was only the reading and receiving of experience. And I had to be open because I had to write it in the diary.

So I would like to remove from everyone the feeling that writing is something that is only done by a few gifted people. I want to eliminate this instantly. ...You shouldn't think that someone who achieves fulfillment in writing and a certain art in writing is necessarily a person with unusual gifts. I always said that it was an unusual stubbornness. Nothing prevented me from doing it every night, after every day's happenings.

It's not only the people with unusual gifts who will write their life in an interesting way. It has nothing to do really with the literary value of the work. What is important is that in the doing of it you begin to penetrate much deeper into the layers of consciousness and the unconscious. I registered everything. I registered intuitions, prophesies; I would be looking into the future or looking back and re-examining the past.

I don't want to make writers of all of you, but I *do* want you to become very aware of your orientation. First of all, of how much contact you have with yourself. If you remember, in the early diaries I spoke of my feelings that I was playing all the roles demanded of woman, which I had been programmed to play. But I knew also that there was a part of myself that stood apart from that and wanted some other kind of life, some other kind of authenticity. R.D. Laing describes this authenticity as a process of constant peeling off the false selves. You can do this in many ways, but you can begin by looking at it, for there is so much that we *don't* want to look at. I didn't want to see exactly where I was in Louveciennes before I made friends, before I entered the literary life, before I wrote my first book. I didn't want to see that I was nowhere, but wanting to see is terribly important to our direction. And to find this direction I used every possible means. Not only friendship and psychology and therapy, but also a tremendous amount of reading, exploration, listening to others—all these things contributed to my discovering who I really was. It wasn't as final or definite as it might sound now, because it doesn't happen in one day and it doesn't happen finally. It's a continuum, it's something that goes on all of your life. But once I was at least on the track of what I could do, then the obstacles began to move away. It was not something that anybody could give me, it was something that I had to find inside myself.

So I'm speaking now of the diary not as a work of literature but as something necessary to living, as a way of orienting ourselves to our inner lives. It doesn't matter in what form you do it, whether it's meditation, whether it's writing or whether it's just a moment of thoughtfulness about the trend, the current, of your life. It's a moment of stopping life in order to become aware of it. And it's this kind of awareness which is threatened in our world today, with its acceleration and with its mechanization.

In his introduction to the first volume of the *Diary,* Gunther Stuhlmann says that my real life as a writer and a woman is contained in the pages of the journal. I should add to this that what I meant by my real life was that, as many people do, I had two roles to play: one in the world, in which I sought to please everyone, in which I sought to inspire, in which I wanted only to give the best of myself, and then the other truth contained in the journal of how I felt about these people I met, how I felt about what was happening. And in some respects this split originated in the philosophy that truth is destructive. At least I believed that certain kinds of truth were destructive, and these demons were going to be kept secret within the journal. What changed my attitude was the realization that these things that I had condemned were actually the most valuable, that the secret and intimate portraits I made of people, as well as of myself, were far deeper and more revealing than these roles that we all play in life. Those who misunderstood the *Diary* were the ones who were so obsessed with the idea that any introspection, any regard for individual growth, any concern with one's personal conflicts was narcissistic. We saw a great deal of these hysterical, mass, unthinking movements in our period because we did give up the self. The self has to merge with collective interests or general humanity, but first of all it has to *exist* in order to be able to make a choice and to make a contribution. The loss of personal identity, this depersonalization, led to a most dangerous state of dehumanization as we have seen from some of the phenomena of American life. The people who turned to the diary in this period turned in order to find the core of themselves or something they could create with, something they could cling to, a basic understanding, a capacity for evaluation, a knowledge of distinction of quality, these things which had been lost in a kind of anonymous mass unthinkingness.

The diary was not published out of nostalgia for the past. I realized at a certain moment that it connected very strongly with contemporary life. I don't think I would have published it if it simply had been memoirs of people who had died and disappeared and vanished and played no role in the present. But I found that the thinking of Rank, the work of Henry Miller, and the very strong influence of Artaud were active in contemporary life. So that the *Diary* is not a *Recherche du Temps Perdu*. It is actually a seeking to unite the past, the present, and the future. My life today is just as it was when I was writing the diary; it is always very full and very rich. I'm always exploring new realms of experience, I'm always curious, I'm always ready for adventure.

I did not wish to recapture the past. But I was elated to find that the things and the people and the places I had loved could remain alive forever. I was pleased to realize that I had awakened to life permanently. This was a discovery which really pushed me into editing the diary. I felt humble about it because I felt that it was not really a biography as much as a portrait of others. Of course it's necessary to be an individual, to be the proper mirror for others. If you have a small mirror you cannot reflect big personalities. In my great effort to perfect myself as a sensitive instrument with a wide range, I made a comparison always to the mirror. The mirror has to have identity and an existence and intelligence in what it records. And of this I am proud in the diary; I did record essential things.

The personal life, deeply lived, takes you beyond the personal. This was the discovery that I made when I relinquished the diary, which was my secret. I discovered that it belonged to everybody, and not only to me.

Instead of being discovered when the *Diary* appeared, it was I who made a discovery, of thousands and thousands of women I didn't know, of a whole segment of American life I didn't know. But this is perhaps the only important thing that fame brings, that it helps you to connect with a wider world. And so I am the one who made a discovery, who discovered you.

A Selective Bibliography of American Autobiography

I. BIBLIOGRAPHIES

Brignano, Russell C., *Black Americans in Autobiography: An Annotated Bibliography of Autobiographies and Autobiographical Books Written Since the Civil War.* Durham N.C.: Duke University Press, 1974.

Kaplan, Louis, *A Bibliography of American Autobiographies.* Madison: University of Wisconsin Press, 1962.

Lillard, Richard, *American Life in Autobiography: A Descriptive Guide.* Stanford: Stanford University Press, 1956.

II. GENERAL WORKS ON AUTOBIOGRAPHY

Allport, Gordon, *The Uses of Personal Documents in Psychological Sciences.* New York: Social Science Research Council, 1942.

Bruss, Elizabeth, *Autobiographical Acts: The Changing Situation of a Literary Genre.* Baltimore: John Hopkins University Press, 1976.

Cooke, Michael G., "'Do You Remember Laura?' or, The Limits of Autobiography," *Iowa Review* 9 (Spring 1978), 58-72.

Dilthey, Wilhelm, *Pattern and Meaning in History,* ed. H.P. Rickman. New York: Harper & Bros., 1962.

Earle, William, *The Autobiographical Consciousness: A Philosophical Inquiry into Existence.* Chicago: Quadrangle Books, 1972.

Erikson, Erik H., *Life History and the Historical Moment.* New York: W.W. Norton & Co., Inc., 1975.

Fothergill, Robert A., *Private Chronicles: A Study of English Diaries.* London: Oxford University Press, 1974.

Gusdorf, Georges, "Conditions and Limits of Autobiography" in *Autobiography: Essays Theoretical and Critical,* ed. J. Olney, pp. 28-48.

Hart, Francis Russell, "Notes for an Anatomy of Modern Autobiography," *New Literary History* 1 (Spring 1970), 485-511.

Howarth, William L., "Some Principles of Autobiography," *New Literary History* 5 (Winter 1974), 363-81.

Howells, William D., "Autobiography, a New Form of Literature," *Harper's Monthly Magazine* 107 (October 1909), 795-98.

Jelinek, Estelle C., ed., *Women's Autobiography: Essays in Criticism.* Bloomington: Indiana University Press, 1980.

Kazin, Alfred, "Autobiography as Narrative," *Michigan Quarterly Review* 3 (Fall, 1964), 210-16.

Langness, L.L., *The Life History in Anthropological Science.* New York: Holt, Rinehart, & Winston, 1965.

Lejeune, Philippe, *Le pacte autobiographique.* Paris: Éditions de Seuil, 1975.

Mandel, Barrett J., "Autobiography: Reflection Trained on Mystery," *Prairie Schooner* 46 (Winter 1972-73), 323-38.

_____, "Full of Life Now," in Olney, *Autobiography: Essays Theoretical and Critical,"* pp. 49-72.

Mazlish, Bruce, "Autobiography and Psycho-Analysis: Between Truth and Self-Deception," *Encounter* 35 (October 1970), 28-37.

Mehlman, Jeffrey, *A Structural Study of Autobiography: Proust, Leiris, Sartre, Lévi-Strauss.* Ithaca: Cornell University Press, 1974.

Morris, John, *Versions of the Self: Studies in English Autobiography from John Bunyan to John Stuart Mill.* New York: Columbia University Press, 1966.

Olney, James, ed., *Autobiography: Essays Theoretical and Critical.* Princeton: Princeton University Press, 1980.

_____, *Metaphors of Self: The Meaning of Autobiography.* Princeton: Princeton University Press, 1972.

_____, *Tell Me Africa: An Approach to African Literature.* Princeton: Princeton University Press, 1973.

Pascal, Roy, *Design and Truth in Autobiography.* Cambridge: Harvard University Press, 1960.

Pike, Burton, "Time in Autobiography," *Comparative Literature* 28 (Fall 1976), 326-42.

Schumaker, Wayne, *English Autobiography: Its Emergence, Materials, and Forms.* Berkeley: University of California Press, 1954.

Shapiro, Steven A., "The Dark Continent of Literature: Autobiography," *Comparative Literature Studies* 5 (December 1968), 421-54.

Smith, Lillian, "Autobiography as a Dialogue between King and Corpse," in *The Winner Names the Age*, ed. M. Cliff, pp. 187-98. New York: W.W. Norton & Co., Inc., 1978.

Spacks, Patricia Meyer, *Imagining a Self: Autobiography and Novel in Eighteenth-Century England*. Cambridge: Harvard University Press, 1976.

———, "Stages of Self: Notes on Autobiography and the Life Cycle," *Boston University Journal* 25, no. 2 (1977), 7-17.

Spender, Stephen, "Confessions and Autobiography," in *The Making of a Poem*, pp. 63-72. New York: W.W. Norton & Co., Inc., 1962.

Spengemann, William C., *The Form of Autobiography: Episodes in the History of a Literary Genre*. New Haven: Yale University Press, 1980.

Starobinski, Jean, "The Style of Autobiography," in *Literary Style: A Symposium*, ed. S. Chatman, pp. 285-94. New York: Oxford University Press, 1971.

Sturrock, John, "The New Model Autobiographer," *New Literary History* 9 (Autumn 1977), 51-63.

Weintraub, Karl J., "Autobiography and Historical Consciousness," *Critical Inquiry* 1 (June 1975), 821-48.

———, *The Value of the Individual: Self and Circumstance in Autobiography*. Chicago: University of Chicago Press, 1978.

III. INTERPRETATIONS OF AMERICAN AUTOBIOGRAPHY

Adams, Timothy D., "The Contemporary American Mock-Autobiography," *Clio* 8 (Spring 1979), 417-28.

Agar, Michael, "Stories, Background Knowledge and Themes: Problems in the Analysis of Life History Narrative," *American Ethnologist* 7 (May 1980), 223-39.

Alkon, Paul, "Visual Rhetoric in *The Autobiography of Alice B. Toklas*," *Critical Inquiry* 1 (June 1975), 849-81.

Arensberg, Liliane K., "Death as Metaphor of Self in *I Know Why the Caged Bird Sings*," *College Language Association Journal* 20 (December 1976), 273-91.

Baker, Houston A., Jr., "Autobiographical Acts and the Voice of the Southern Slave," in *The Journey Back: Issues in Black Literature and Criticism,* 27-52. Chicago: University of Chicago Press, 1980.

Barton, Rebecca Chalmers, *Witnesses for Freedom: Negro Americans in Autobiography.* Oakdale, N.Y.: Dowling College Press, 1976.

Beidler, Philip, "Franklin and Crèvecoeur's 'Literary' Americans," *Early American Literature* 13 (Spring, 1978), 193-212.

Berthoff, Warner, "Witness and Testament: Two Contemporary Classics," *New Literary History* 2 (Winter 1971), 311-27; reprinted in *Aspects of Narrative,* ed. J. Hillis Miller, 173-198. New York: Columbia University Press,1971. [Concerning Malcolm X, Mailer]

Billson, Marcus, and Sidonie Smith, "Lillian Hellman and the Strategy of the 'Other,'" in *Women's Autobiography,* ed. E. Jelinek, 163-79.

Blackburn, Regina, "In Search of the Black Female Self: African-American Women's Autobiographies and Ethnicity," in *Women's Autobiography,* ed. E. Jelinek, 133-48.

Blackmur, Richard, P., *Henry Adams.* New York: Harcourt Brace Jovanovich, 1980.

Blasing, Mutlu Konuk, *The Art of Life: Studies in American Autobiographical Literature.* Austin: University of Texas Press, 1977.

Blassingame, John W., "Black Autobiographies as History and Literature," *Black Scholar* 5 (December 1973-January 1974), 2-9.

Bloom, Lynn Z., "Gertrude Is Alice Is Everybody: Innovation and Point of View in Gertrude Stein's Autobiographies," *Twentieth Century Literature* 24 (Spring 1978), 81-93.

Bridgman, Richard, *trude Stein in Pieces.* New York: Oxford University Press, 1970.

Bruchac, Joseph, "Black Autobiography in Africa and America," *Black Academy Review* 2 (1977), 61-70.

Buell, Lawrence, "Transcendentalist Self-Examination and Autobiographical Tradition," in *Literary Transcendentalism: Style and Vision in the American Renaissance.* Ithaca: Cornell University Press, 1973.

Bushman, Richard, "On the Uses of Psychology: Conflict and Conciliation in Benjamin Franklin," *History and Theory* 5 (1966), 255-40.

Burger, Mary W., "I, Too, Sing America: The Black Autobiographer's Response to Life in the Midwest and Mid-Plains," *Kansas Quarterly* 7 (Summer 1975), 43-57.

Butterfield, Stephen, *Black Autobiography in America.* Amherst: University of Massachusetts Press, 1974.

Cobb, Edith, "The Ecology of Imagination in Childhood," *Daedalus* 88 (Summer 1959), 537-48.

Cooke, Michael G., "Modern Black Autobiography in the Tradition," in *Romanticism: Vistas, Instances, Continuities,* eds. D. Thorburn and G. Hartman. Ithaca: Cornell University Press, 1973.

Cooley, Thomas, *Educated Lives: The Rise of Modern Autobiography in America.* Columbus: Ohio State University Press, 1976.

Couser, G. Thomas, *American Autobiography: The Prophetic Mode.* Amherst: University of Massachusetts Press, 1979.

———, "The Shape of Death in American Autobiography," *Hudson Review* 31 (Spring 1978), 53-66.

Cox, James M., "Autobiography and America," in *Aspects of Narrative,* ed. J. Hillis Miller, 143-72. New York: Columbia University Press, 1971.

———, "Autobiography and Washington," *Sewanee Review* 85 (April-June 1977), 235-61.

———, "Jefferson's *Autobiography:* Recovering Literature's Lost Ground," *Southern Review* 14 (October 1978), 633-52.

Demarest, David P., "*The Autobiography of Malcolm X:* Beyond Didacticism," *College Language Association Journal* 16 (December 1972), 179-87.

Eakin, Paul John, "Alfred Kazin's Bridge to .America," *South Atlantic Quarterly* 77 (Winter 1978), 81-93.

———, "Malcolm X and the Limits of Autobiography," *Criticism* 18 (Summer 1976), 230-42.

Fendelman, Earl, "Toward Walden Pond: The American Voice in Autobiography," *Canadian Review of American Studies* 8 (Spring 1977), 11-25.

Gilman, Richard, *The Confusion of Realms,* (New York: Random House, Inc., 1970) [Malcolm X, Cleaver, Mailer] 3-21, 81-153.

Greenacre, Phyllis, *Emotional Growth: Psychoanalytic Studies of the Gifted and a Great Variety of Other Individuals* (Vol. II). New York: International University Press, 1971.

Gunn, Janet Varner, "Autobiography and the Narrative Experience of Temporality as Depth," *Soundings* 60 (Summer 1977), 194-209.

Haerle, R.K., Jr., "Athlete as 'Moral' Leader: Heroes, Success Themes, and Basic Cultural Values in Selected Baseball Autobiographies, 1900-1970," *Journal of Popular Culture* 8 (Fall 1974), 392-401,

Harbert, Earl N., "Henry Adams's *Education* and the Autobiographical Tradition," *Tulane Studies in English* 22 (1977), 133-41.

Hart, Francis Russell, "History Talking to Itself: Public Personality in Recent Memoir," *New Literary History* 11 (Autumn 1979), 193-210.

Hoffa, William, "The Final Preface: Henry James's Autobiography," *Sewanee Review* 77 (Spring 1969), 277-93.

Holly, Carol T., "*Black Elk Speaks* and the Making of Indian Autobiography," *Genre* 12 (Spring 1979), 117-36.

Horowitz, Irving L., "Autobiography as Presentation of Self for Social Immortality," *New Literary History* 9 (Autumn 1977) 173-79.

Hurt, James, "Walden on Halsted Street: Jane Addams' *Twenty Years at Hull House,*" *Centennial Review* 23 (Spring 1979), 185-207.

Juhasz, Suzanne, "Towards a Theory of Form in Feminist Autobiography: Kate Mullett's *Flying* and *Sita;* Maxine Hong Kingston's *The Woman Warrior,*" in *Women's Autobiography,* ed. E. Jelinek, 221-37.

Kazin, Alfred, "The Self as History: Reflections on Autobiography," in *Telling Lives: The Biographer's Art,* ed. M. Pachter, pp. 74-80. Washington: New Republic Books, 1979.

Kent, George E., "Maya Angelou's *I Know Why the Caged Bird Sings* and Black Autobiographical Tradition," *Kansas Quarterly* 7 (Summer 1975), 72-78.

Leibowitz, Herbert, "Stoking the Oedipal Furnace: Edward Dahlberg's *Because I Was Flesh,*" *American Scholar* 44 (Summer 1975), 473-83.

Lemay, J.A. Leo, "Franklin and the *Autobiography:* An Essay on Recent Scholarship," *Eighteenth-Century Studies* 1 (December 1967), 185-211.

Levenson, J.C., *The Mind and Art of Henry Adams.* Stanford: Stanford University Press, 1968.

Levin, David, "Baldwin's Autobiographical Essays: The Problem of Negro Identity," in *Black and White in American Culture,* eds. J. Chametzky and S. Kaplin, pp. 372-79. Amherst: University of Massachusetts Press, n.d.

————, *In Defense of Historical Literature: Essays on American History, Autobiography, Drama, and Fiction.* New York: Hill & Wang, 1967. [Frankl,j]

Lynen, John, *The Design of the Present: Essays on Time and Form in American Literature*, 87-152. New Haven: Yale University Press, 1969. [Edwards, Franklin]

Mandel, Barrett J., "The Didactic Achievement of Malcolm X's *Autobiography,*" *Afro-American Studies* 2 (March 1972), 269-74.

Martin, Jay, *Conrad Aiken: The Life of His Art.* Princeton: Princeton University Press, 1962.

McCluskey, Sally, "Black Elk Speaks—And So Does John Neihardt," *Western American Literature* 6 (Winter 1972), 231-42.

Miller, Henry, "Une Être Étoilique," in *Cosmological Eye*, 269-91. New York: New Directions, 1939. [Nin]

Miller, Ross, "Autobiography as Fact and Fiction: Franklin, Adams, Malcolm X," *Centennial Review* 16 (Summer 1972), 221-32.

Minter, David, "By Dens of Lions: Notes on Stylization in Early Puritan Captivity Narratives," *American Literature* 45 (November 1973), 335-47.

————, "Conceptions of Self in Black Slave Narratives," *American Transcendental Quarterly* 24 (1974), 62-68.

————, *The Interpreted Design as a Structural Principle in American Prose.* New Haven: Yale University Press, 1969.

Nichols, Charles H., *Many Thousand Gone: The Ex-Slaves' Account of Their Bondage and Freedom.* Bloomington: Indiana University Press, 1969.

Nichols, W.W., "Slave Narratives: Dismissed Evidence in the Writing of Southern History," *Phylon* 32 (Winter 1971), 403-09.

O'Brien, Lynn W., *Plains Indian Autobiographies.* Boise: Boise State College, 1973.

Ohmann, Carol, "*The Autobiography of Malcolm X:* A Revolutionary Use of the Franklin Tradition," *American Quarterly* 22 (Summer 1970), 131-49.

Olney, James, "Autos*Bios*Graphein: The Study of Autobiographical Literature," *South Atlantic Quarterly* 77 (Winter 1978), 113-23.

Porter, Roger J., "Emptying His Sock of Woe: Edward Dahlberg's *Because I Was Flesh,*" *Contemporary Literature* 18 (Spring 1977), 141-59.

————, "Unspeakable Practices, Writable Acts: Franklin's *Autobiography,*" *Hudson Review* 32 (Summer 1979), 224-38.

Rainer, Tristine, "Anaïs Nin's *Diary I:* The Birth of the Young Woman as an Artist," in *A Casebook of Anaïs Nin,* ed. Robert Zaller, 161-68. New York: New American Library, 1974.

Rosenblatt, Roger, "Black Autobiography: Life as the Death Weapon," *Yale Review* 65 (June 1976), 515-27; reprinted in *Autobiography: Essays Theoretical and Critical,* ed. J. Olney, 169-80.

Rubin, Louis D., "The Self Observed," *Kenyon Review* 35 (Summer 1962), 393-415.

Sayre, Robert F., "Autobiography and Images of Utopia," *Salmagundi* 19 (Spring 1972), 18-37.

———, "Autobiography and the Making of America," in Olney, *Autobiography: Essays Theoretical and Critical,* 146-68.

———, *The Examined Self: Benjamin Franklin, Henry Adams, Henry James.* Princeton: Princeton University Press, 1964.

———, "The Proper Study: Autobiographies in American Studies," *American Quarterly* 29 (Bibliography Issue, 1977), 241-62.

———, "Vision and Experience in *Black Elk Speaks,*" *College English* 32 (February 1971), 509-35.

Schlissel, Lillian, "Women's Diaries on the Western Frontier," *American Studies* 18 (Spring 1977), 87-100.

Schultz, Elizabeth, "To Be Black and Blue: The Blues Genre in Black American Autobiography," *Kansas Quarterly* 7 (Summer 1975), 81-96.

Shea, Daniel B., Jr., *Spiritual Autobiography in Early America.* Princeton: Princeton University Press, 1968.

Slotkin, Richard, *Regeneration through Violence.* Middletown, Conn.: Wesleyan University Press, 1973. [Captivity narratives, slave narratives]

Smith, Sidonie, *Where I'm Bound: Patterns of Slavery and Freedom in Black American Autobiography.* Westport, Conn.: Greenwood Press, 1974. (See also Billson, Marcus.)

Smith, William F., Jr., "American Indian Autobiographies," *American Indian Quarterly* 2 (Autumn 1975), 237-45.

Spacks, Patricia Meyer, "Selves in Hiding," in *Women's Autobiography,* ed. E. Jelinek, 112-32.

Spengemann, W.C., and L.R. Lundquist, "Autobiography and the American Myth," *American Quarterly* 17 (Fall 1965), 501-19.

Steiner, Wendy, *Exact Resemblance to Exact Resemblance: The Literary Portraiture of Gertrude Stein.* New Haven: Yale University Press, 1978.

Stepto, Robert B., *From Behind the Veil: A Study of Afro-American Narrative.* Urbana, Ill.: University of Illinois Press, 1979.

Stinson, Robert, "S.S. McClure's *My Autobiography:* The Progressive as Self-Made Man," *American Quarterly* 22 (Summer 1970), 203-12.

Stone, Albert E., "After *Black Boy* and *Duck of Dawn:* Patterns in Recent Black Autobiography," *Phylon* 39 (March 1978), 18-34.

———, "Autobiography and American Culture," *American Studies: An International Newsletter* 11 (December 1972), 22-36; reprinted in *American Studies: Topics & Sources,* ed. Robert H. Walker, 22-37. Westport, Conn.: Greenwood Press, 1976.

———, "Autobiography and the Childhood of the American Artist: The Example of Louis Sullivan," in *American Character and Culture in a Changing World,* ed. John A. Hague, 294-332. Westport, Conn.: Greenwood Press, 1980.

———, "Cato's Mirror: The Face of Violence in American Autobiography," in *Prospects: An Annual of American Cultural Studies* (Vol. III), ed. Jack Salzman, 331-60. New York: Burt Franklin & Co., 1977.

———, "Identity and Art in Frederick Douglass's *Narrative,*" *College Language Association Journal* 17 (December 1973), 192-213.

———, "The Sea and the Self: Travel as Experience and Metaphor in Early American Literature," *Genre* 7 (September 1974), 279-306.

Tintner, Adeline R., "Autobiography as Fiction: The Usurping Consciousness as Hero of James's Memoirs," *Twentieth-Century Literature* 23 (May 1977), 239-60.

Ward, John William, "Violence, Anarchy, and Alexander Berkman," *New York Review of Books* 15 (November 5, 1970), 25-30.

———, "Who Was Benjamin Franklin?" *American Scholar* 32 (Autumn 1963), 541-53.

Waddle, David L., "The Image of Self in Jonathan Edwards: A Study of Autobiography and Theology," *American Academy of Religion Journal* 43 (March 1975), 70-83.

White, Ralph K., "*Black Boy:* A Value Analysis," *Journal of Abnormal and Social Psychology* 42 (October 1947), 440-61.

Whitfield, Stephen J., "Three Masters of Impression Management: Benjamin Franklin, Booker T. Washington, and Malcom X as Autobiographers," *South Atlantic Quarterly* 77 (Autumn 1978), 399-417.

Zaller, Robert, *A Casebook on Anaïs Nin.* New York: New American Library, 1974.

Zavarzadek, Mas'ud, *The Mythopoeic Reality: The Postwar American Nonfictional Novel* (Urbana, Ill.: University of Illinois Press, 1976.

Notes on the Editor and Contributors

ALBERT E. STONE is Professor of English and Chairman of American Studies at the University of Iowa. He is the author of *The Innocent Eye: Childhood in Mark Twain's Imagination*, (1961) and editor of Crèvecoeur's *Letters From An American Farmer and Sketches of XVIII-Century America* (1963; revised edition forthcoming). He is completing a book tentatively entitled *Autobiographical Occasions and Original Acts: Studies in Modern American Autobiography*.

ROBERT F. SAYRE is Professor of English at the University of Iowa. He is the author of two books, *The Examined Self: Benjamin Franklin, Henry Adams, Henry James* (1964) and *Thoreau and the American Indians* (1977). Besides autobiography, his interests include Native American literature. He is currently making an experiment in family and personal history.

ALFRED KAZIN, Distinguished Professor of English at the City University of New York, is the author of a notable series of books critical, biographical, and autobiographical. These include *On Native Grounds: An Interpretation of Modern American Literature* (1942); *A Walker in the City* (1951); *Starting Out in the Thirties* (1965); *Bright Book of Life* (1973); and *New York Jew* (1978).

PATRICIA MEYER SPACKS, Professor of English at Yale University, is the author of *The Young Idea: Social Mythologies of Adolescence, 1740-1960*, to be published in 1981 by Basic Books. She has written about English autobiography in *Imagining a Self* (1976).

DARREL MANSELL is Professor of English at Dartmouth College. The author of *The Novels of Jane Austen*, numerous articles on George Eliot (one appears in the Spectrum Book on George Eliot), and various articles on Shakespeare, Keats, Jane Austen, Ernest Hemingway, and critical theory, he is currently writing a book on the theory of metaphor.

JANET VARNER GUNN is currently Visiting Assistant Professor of Religious Studies at the University of North Carolina at Greensboro. She taught previously at North Park College in Chicago. Her interests lie in religion and literature and her book on autobiography is forthcoming at the University of Pennsylvania Press.

THOMAS P. DOHERTY received undergraduate degrees in English and political science from Gonzaga University in 1974. He is currently a Ph.D. candidate in American Studies at the University of Iowa.

ELIZABETH SCHULTZ, Professor of English at the University of Kansas, has also taught at the University of Michigan, Tuskegee Institute, and various universities in Japan. She has published on Henry James, Afro-American literature, and Japanese literature, in addition to short stories and translations.

ALVIN H. ROSENFELD is Professor of English and Director of Jewish Studies at Indiana University. He is the author of *A Double Dying: Reflections on Holocaust Literature* (1980) and co-editor of *Confronting the Holocaust: The Impact of Elie Wiesel* (1979), among other works.

ANAÏS NIN died in 1977 after a long and distinguished career, of which the first fruits were *The Diary of Anaïs Nin* in six volumes. She was also a novelist—*House of Incest* (1936); *Winter of Artifice* (1934); *Cities of the Interior* (1959); *Collages* (1964)— a psychoanalyst, and a critic.

INDEX